HOW GRIM WAS MY VALLEY

CHRIS GRIFFITHS

EDITED BY PATRICIA HILTON-JOHNSON

*First print
A donation will be made from profits of this book to a local women's
refuge charity.*

ISBN-13: 978-1492282020
ISBN-10: 1492282022

Dedicated to my mum who has had a long and hard journey.

WITH SPECIAL THANKS TO:

Patricia Griffiths, Adrian Magson,
Caroline Rushton, Pippin, Mark & Phill
and for all those people who are no longer with us.

Contents

Preface

The story that follows is slightly more than just a list of anecdotes, but also an insight into a boy who was raised in the 1960s and 1970s, and how he coped with the rigours of everyday life amidst the working classes. This book is not intended to offend or hurt anybody; however, I am sure it will. You will soon realise that I am not an author.

Within the working classes there seemed to be a tradition of turning hardship into laughter. By writing this book I hope to show that even at the lowest moments of our lives we can usually manage to cope, and come through the other side a little wiser. It is about nobody special, just an ordinary boy who was raised in a village called Weedon Bec in the county of Northamptonshire, England.

As you will no doubt notice, I have mainly illustrated the book with postcards that I have sourced from as far afield as the U.S.A. This is because I have limited access to photographs. Obviously the dates on the cards vary, but most of the scenery remains.

This account may remind people of some of the lighter moments in life, and I again apologise if I write about memories that they wanted to forget.

Chapter 1

Why we lived in Weedon

Plenty of hardship,
Prospects were slim.
Children a plenty,
In the valley so grim.

Weedon Bec is situated at the centre of England within the county of Northamptonshire. The majority of the village is down in the valley. In the past few hundred years it has been home to the Normans, Romans, Danes and many, many others, perhaps attracted by the local pubs and stunning wenches?

In the early 1800s large military buildings were erected, and used for barracks, ordnance stores and a small military prison. These buildings were surrounded by enormous walls and towers. The main entrances consisted of large gates, a canal, portcullis and a railway line. Some of the buildings were originally built to house the royal family if the country was invaded by the French, this of course didn't happen because we, as usual, duffed them up.

During the next 150 years tens of thousands of troops passed through the barracks, and millions of munitions were stored there. It later became a government stores and remained as that until the 1980s.

Because of the military background Weedon was an unusual village. All the kids were of different shapes, sizes, hair colourings and accents. Most of the kids were the offspring of squaddies; nearly all our fathers and grandfathers had been in the forces.

In the 1930s and 1940s the village held dozens of pubs, frequented by many hardened servicemen; thus, street fights were commonplace.

My maternal grandfather spent twenty years in the Bedfordshire and Hertfordshire regiment and twenty-two years in the War department police. He was a giant of a man, with a barrel chest and booming voice, and Weedon was to be his final posting. He lived in police quarters near the main road with his two daughters, Ethel (my mum) and Anne (my auntie). My maternal grandmother had passed away in 1936 when my mother was seven years old. This led to an extremely hard and loveless childhood, as she was pushed into a convent school. My grandfather eventually married again, this time to his step-daughter (my mum's half-sister). The daughter from my grandmothers first marriage. And yes I know it was very complicated. My mother had a very unhappy time, and when her stepmother died she was left to raise her younger sister Anne. Her father drank to excess and beat my poor mum regularly.

My father, Hugh Lloyd Griffiths, was born in Caernarfon, North Wales, in 1917. He was one of eleven children who resided in a rented two-up, two-down terraced house. His mother had passed away when he was a small child, and his father sent him to work on a hill farm at the age of twelve.

My father educated himself and held numerous jobs until war broke out. He and his brothers all joined the Royal Welch Fusiliers. Hugh was sent to the Far East and spent the entire war fighting the Japanese. When finally he returned he was extremely ill. He left Wales in 1949 and moved to Northampton, to live with his uncle who was blinded in the First World War. It was here he met his future wife Ethel. After six weeks of courtship they married and lived with my maternal grandfather in the police house.

In 1951 my eldest brother Paul was born, followed by my sister Gwyneth in 1953. My grandfather retired at this point and they all moved to a council house at 35 Newcroft, on to one of the large estates. It was there in 1959 that my brother Neville was born, and then in 1961 my brother Andrew. The seven of them then moved to another council house in Queens Park where I was born in 1963. My brothers have said that I was such an ugly baby that when I was born the doctor smacked my mum.

In 1966, when I was three years old, we moved again,

this time to Number 8 Newcroft; here my baby sister was born in 1968. The majority of people in Newcroft were in the same boat, they lived in overcrowded conditions with never enough money. Shortly after this move my grandfather died in St Crispin's Mental Hospital. I hope it was nothing to do with me.

Many of the local adults were still suffering from the effects of the wars. Even as a child I realised that life was not fair. During the war certain people in reserved occupations bought property at cheap rates, never got bombed and had a wonderful post war experience. How can that compare with the trauma that was suffered by my grandfathers and father and many like them? My dad was one of the many thousands who came home to nothing, and many not living long enough to pick up their well-earned pensions.

1063   THE BARRACKS, WEEDON.

The Ordnance depot where my maternal grandfather and my father worked.
We eventually moved here.

Chapter 2
Number 8 Newcroft

A crowded house,
With plenty of fears.
Too many screams,
And too many tears.

My earliest recollection was in 1966 at the age of three, which
happened to be the day that we moved from Queens Park. I
was sitting on my dad's shoulders crossing the playing field in
Upper Weedon. Our new council home was built in the 1950s
and was a solidly built semi-detached house, one of many on
the estate. What was most important for my mother and father
was that the house had an inside toilet. Oh, what a luxury. I
couldn't understand what all the excitement was about, but
then again it didn't really concern me, as I was still going to the
toilet in my pants.

The three small bedrooms were divided up between
Paul (aged fifteen), Gwyn (aged thirteen), Neville (aged seven),
Andrew (aged five) and me. We were considered to be a
normal working-class family, who had bugger all. My dad
regularly suffered with his malaria, breathing and various other
illnesses, due to his time in Burma, but always tried to work
hard to bring money into the house.

Money was always tight and my mother struggled to keep a home, six children and numerous pets. My Esso petrol football coin collection was in and out the meter more than the repair man was. The collection of these coins was really an amazing achievement, as we never had a car. Our large collection of candles was always close to hand, just in case we got cut off or if there was a power cut, which was a regular occurrence. If it was timed right the estate could look very festive all year-round.

My parents were of a generation that if a child misbehaved he or she deserved a good hiding; this instilled a sense of survival in me, and taught me to become crafty. Where there is a large family there is always a runt, unfortunately this was me, as my mother recently reminded me.

On regular occasions my elder brothers would make me put on my boxing gloves and fight my older, bigger brother Andrew. Unfortunately we only had one pair of gloves so Andrew would have to wear my mum's mittens. My gum shield was a piece of cardboard and my head guard was the tea cosy, and under Neville's guidance (he was my cut man and trainer) I would get in close and throw a few useful body shots, so as to bring on an asthma attack. The outcome, however, was inevitable as Andrew would remove the mittens and hit me with his bare knuckles on top of my head. This was affectionately known as a nut cracker and would bring on floods of tears.

The estate kids would squabble and fight with each other, as did the adults; it was a normal part of our life. My parents argued daily, and this always ended up with Mum screaming and throwing things at my father. Fortunately for Dad she was a poor aim, so much so that one day she missed him completely and threw a china egg cup into my face. It smashed just above my eye, and a neighbour had to rush me to hospital. I received six stitches and was given two sweets by the nurse for not crying. At the hospital I was taken into a room and questioned by a woman from social services. She wanted to know how it happened. I of course gave her a dramatic, graphic account of how I was running like a gazelle, tripped and caught my eye on the settee. I wasn't going to entrust our family secrets with a woman who sounded that posh. Anyway it got me two weeks off school. The next day my big sister Gwyn was there to comfort me as usual, and bring me a toy.

These things didn't just happen in our house, they happened all over the estate. Poverty and overcrowding caused people to behave irrationally. When I was five, Gwyn, who was sixteen, eloped to Gretna Green with a much older man and got married. Paul left shortly after that and joined the police force. He is still with them, more than thirty years later, what an achievement.

When Gwyn was eighteen, she had a baby son called David, and her struggle began in earnest. During the next three years she periodically separated from her violent husband and came to stay with us. Little David and my younger sister Ceri were both very young, so automatically formed a special bond, which is still there. Many times Gwyn's estranged husband would break into our house and beat up Gwyn. On one such occasion, my tiny 5-foot, 6-stone dad tried to stop him, got knocked to the ground and had his nose broken by the bigger, nastier, violent man. Even with these injuries my dad got back up and tried to stop Gwyn's husband from stealing a screaming David. The police were called and eventually persuaded the thug to return the baby to Gwyn. All charges were dropped because it was considered a domestic.

The following week Gwyn and baby David were in our house when the door was kicked open and her husband entered and beat the living daylights out of her. She was sobbing in agony, and all I could do was cower behind Dad's chair, crying. My older brothers, Andy and Neville, and I (at age seven) were too frightened to move; we couldn't protect her. I have to live with the fact that I did nothing. I was a coward. As a child I hoped I would lose my memory and never have to think about it again, but this wasn't to be. That day a part of Gwyn died. Her husband made her go back and live with him.

The next day Gwyn came round the house with presents for us. She bought us these as an apology, as she felt guilty for being beaten in front of us. The bruises she carried were black, green, brown, grey, blue and purple. I have never seen anything like it since. I felt so hurt and sorry for her and again the police did nothing. When I asked her why she had to go back to him she replied in a croaky voice, "Because I have to".

In 1973 (when I was ten) Gwyn left her husband for the final time. She moved into a council house in Queen Street, but came home daily to scrounge fags off Dad or give us haircuts. It was during these visits from Gwyn that I realised how close we had become, and I looked forward to them.

As fights among the local kids were commonplace, it was not unusual when a couple of dozen of us were playing over the field one day, and two unknown lads appeared. I don't know how it started but I was stripped to the waist and was squaring up to the bigger of the two boys, who was taller and stockier than me. My brother, however, thought it would be a good fight. Within seconds the local kids had formed a large circle around the two of us, and had prepared us for battle like two fighting cocks.

I fought with the stranger for hours, or at least twenty minutes, and was covered in his and my blood. He knocked me down time and time again, and each time I was picked up, sobbing, and forced back into the fray. After a dozen or so times the other lad, who I now know to be called Paul, gave up. He knew that no matter how many times he knocked me down I could never give in. Years later I bumped into him at senior school and the matter was never discussed. This was just as well because he became a serious body builder who beat the local arm wrestling champion. He was a massive bugger.

After this battle I decided to avoid fighting and throw myself into alternative activities. I saw myself more as a lover than a fighter. It is a pity the local girls didn't agree. I still carry the bruises from where they would push me away with a 10-foot barge pole.

The remainder of our time at 8 Newcoft remained relatively trouble free, although I attended hospital on quite a few occasions, usually due to clumsiness. I did, however, nearly die once. My temperature was sky high and I couldn't stop vomiting, so they rushed me to hospital and cut me open. I still think someone poisoned me. After a stay in the isolation ward

I was released; they never found out what was wrong with me. Gwyn arranged for me to be picked up from the hospital and brought home. When I was carried, wrapped in a blanket into the front room of our house, I saw, to my horror, Andrew and Neville playing with my Airfix toy soldiers. They couldn't even wait for my body to go cold. Talk about vultures picking over the carcass.

Another memorable hospital visit was when I had my tonsils removed. This time I took precautions and hid my toy soldiers in the garden and took my football sticker book into hospital with me. After surgery I awoke to find that a thieving git in the next bed had nicked some of my stickers, I was sure I could have beaten him up, but I just burst into floods of tears at the sheer unfairness of it all. These stickers had been so difficult for me to collect, and Gwyn and I had spent many hours pasting them with flour and water into my book. My tiny tears impression took the thief by surprise so he gave them back to me. When I returned home my toy soldiers had been stolen from the garden, I again realised how much life was unfair.

It wasn't just sad memories that surround 8 Newcroft, there were some special ones, as well. In the 1950s my mother took Paul, Gwyn and Neville (in a pram) up to Everdon Stubbs (the bluebell woods), so it was a delight for us when she carried on the tradition and took Neville, Andrew, Ceri (in the pram) and me up there in the 1960s.

I still remember that special day as clear as any. It was sunny, and it was a good six-mile-round trip walk. All the bluebells were out, and we took Granddad's old gramophone and marching band records. We ate jam sandwiches and drank orange squash. It was the most beautiful place on earth. We had the entire woods to play in and nobody was arguing. The ground was like a blue carpet and the smell was wonderful. We walked the three miles home, contented and exhausted. In those days you were allowed to pick the bluebells, so we filled the pram up with them and put them all over the house. It was sad to see them wither and die. Many years later my brother Neville and his wife had two daughters, one they called Daisy and the other they called Bluebell.

I still return every year with my wife Patricia and my dog Pippin, and we take our sandwiches and drink. When I think about the sacred place I have to have a selective memory, because this is where most of the local lads lost their virginity.

Top right-hand corner of postcard was my first home.

The hospital where I was born; I visited on numerous occasions.

Chapter 3

Circus

Roll up, roll up,
Come take a peek.
Show me your money,
And I'll show you a freak.

It soon became apparent to everyone that I had an obsession with making money. My motto was, "If it moves, sell it". I got to a stage where I was selling all my brothers belongings and sometimes even household goods. I discovered at a very early age that I had an addictive nature. I found that I was hooked on four-for-a-penny blackjack and fruit salad chews; they were my choice of drug. I was sure wars could have been fought over them. I was probably the only kid in the world to extract his milk teeth prematurely, so that the chews would last longer. I would do anything to feed my cravings, and I mean anything.

One bright sunny morning I woke up startled by my first major eureka moment. The previous evening I had been looking at the pictures in one of my brother's Guinness book of records and I saw some of the most fantastic sights ever. They were freak show pictures, and they were brilliant. That gave me the inspirational idea of opening my own circus and displaying my own freak show. I would have liked to have shown the public the ugly faces on my brothers, but they would have been too frightening for my audience, so instead I employed the services of my trusty dogs, Honey and Jenny.

Honey was a lovely, smelly old cocker spaniel, who I felt had a wonderfully artistic temperament: she was loud and volatile. She had entered into our family as a small puppy when her previous owners had mistreated her. They had in fact blinded her in one eye. Jenny was my darling little mongrel dog who went with me everywhere. I loved her more than I loved my brothers. She was extremely docile and loyal and only had three legs. I never knew where her missing leg went, and I never thought to ask. Those two dogs seemed to fit into our estate perfectly.

I soon began touting all the kids who could afford the entrance fee of half a penny, or the kids who I thought might be able to pay me with toy soldiers. The big opening day arrived and I was the money taker, the usher, the compere and the ringmaster.

I began by greeting my excited, ratty-arsed guests at the garden gate, and then led them to the luxury front row seats. Those seats were in fact the hard surface of the garden. Fortunately for them I had removed most of the dog muck from the grass, and of course all entrance fees were collected. Oh, what a professional service I gave.

I wore the kitchen curtain as a cape and my mother's bonnet as my top hat, and the soon-to-be-bored audience sat in amazement when I showed them my star act, which was Honey and Jenny plonked on top of my mother's hall table. You can see by the following photograph that they were professionals, but it soon became apparent that my show was flopping.

Every single one of those philistines began booing and jeering, and some of them had the cheek to ask for their money back. Obviously I couldn't do that as I had overheads to cover. The mini audience turned ugly, and two of the larger art critics broke from the group and began pushing and shoving me. Now that was a serious mistake, because Honey, within the blink of an eye (obviously not her missing one), leapt like a lion from the table and pounced on one of the kids. Her teeth went straight into his backside and his screams were heard on the neighbouring estates. Within seconds all the kids were running, screaming and leaping for safety, and this made Honey even madder. She started chasing everyone. I have never seen a crowd disperse like that; those kids flew our gates and fence like seasoned athletes. This was a memorable lesson in why one should never work with children or animals.

I should have employed my mum as the fortune teller, but instead of me having my palm read she made my arse red.

She had thought that the circus dream was a preferable money maker to what I had been doing, which was that for a small fee I had previously been showing the local girls my little willy. I am sure I could be lured out of retirement for a fee.

Me at the age of three or four. Honey was the spaniel with one eye, and my beloved Jenny who had three legs. They were my best friends.

My brilliant circus.

Chapter 4

Kindness doesn't always pay

He cried, "Flowers for all",
"Equality for the dead".
But instead he was belted,
And sent off to bed.

At the age of three I bumped into my lifetime soul mate, or should I say he bumped into me. His name was Micky Mills. He was a scruffy kid (like me) with curly hair, big lips and big teeth. He could eat an apple through a letter box with his teeth, but he seems to have grown into them now. He lived on the other side of the road to our house.

I was hanging on to my fence, peering over the top like a chad when he came flying passed my garden gate, sitting on a toy tractor. With no sense of fear he crashed straight into my fence. We exchanged swear words and then became best friends. We became little sods immediately.

One sunny morning at the age of four, Micky and I decided to go on one of our many excursions alongside the Grand Union canal, and we eventually ended up in the graveyard opposite to where the old wartime military polo field used to be. This was a very secluded place, where we were left to our own amusement. The only noises were from the birds and the odd train passing nearby. After wandering around the cemetery for an hour, chasing the rabbits, we noticed that a great injustice had been committed. Some of the graves had big, luxurious headstones, regal vases, massive wreaths and wonderful fresh flowers, yet many, like my granddad's had nothing. So we decided to right this wrong. We spent hours rearranging the cemetery. We swapped over some of the smaller headstones, carefully lifting them from one grave to another, distributing all the wreaths and flowers equally and filling all the vases with water. We even scattered the shiny glass stones everywhere. It looked perfect.

It felt like we had been working there for a lifetime, so we decided to take a well-earned rest and admire our handiwork. Because we were too young to read and write, the names on the stones meant nothing to us. We just thought it was sad that all these old people were dead, and that there wasn't anyone to put flowers on their graves. We never thought we were doing anything wrong.

We were so pleased with our first attempt at architectural design that we missed someone watching us. It was in fact Mrs Robinson, who lived two hundred yards away from us on our estate. She had discovered that that her recently deceased mother's stone had been removed, and had rushed to inform my mother.

To this day neighbours still state that my mother covered the mile or so distance from our house to the graveyard in six minutes flat. She moved so fast that we didn't see her charging up the graveyard towards us, like an angry bull elephant. She dragged me by my hair and marched me back to the safe haven of the estate. Micky dragged his heels behind us until we were near his house, and then his mum called him in for his tea. He got off scot-free and I received a double helping of punishment. (He still states that I was the brains of the outfit and he was the brawn, which may have been true ninety percent of the time, but I can assure you that I was punished ninety percent more than he was.)

I was dragged from door to door and made to apologise to everyone in our street, and I was severely thrashed in front of every neighbour. I then realised how big the Newcroft estate was. I was devastated and heartbroken, and I was sobbing so much that I couldn't get my breath, so I couldn't explain why we had done this terrible thing. The only time I ever received worse physical pain from my mother was when she dug abscesses out of my mouth with a hair grip. The physical pain was awful but the emotional pain was far worse. Eventually I was dragged home and belted again for good measure, until Gwyn intervened and scooped me up and comforted me. The slapping had stopped but I wished I was dead. Gwyn was no more than a kid herself but she was my protective big sister.

Years later my brother Neville said that Mum felt awful when she discovered that my act was in fact a charitable gesture not a malicious act. Even at that early age I likened myself to a puppy: if you did wrong and got a deserved clip for it, fair enough, you gave respect. If you were unfairly beaten, however, you just feared them.

On a much lighter note, they say that people are still praying at the wrong graves. I avoided the cemetery for many years, but I knew I had to get revenge on Micky for leaving me to suffer the consequences on my own. It took a little time, but in chapter six revenge was sweet.

The place where we committed the terrible crime.

Part of our journey to the cemetery.

Part of our journey to the cemetery.

Chapter 5

Holiday time

The chalet is empty,
It is seven o'clock.
Stop picking your nose,
And begin picking the lock.

It was strange how my mother's moral stance was soon to change, as even more desperation and fear entered her life. Those two factors can drive people to do some incredible things.

It was during our time at 8 Newcroft that I realised that my mum and dad were very unhappy. They argued constantly, and mum was downtrodden. It was a typically old-fashioned marriage. My dad felt that if he worked hard and brought home the money, that my mother should do everything else. This is not a criticism; it was just the way things were then.

He would expect to come home to a made dinner, bills paid, tidy house and peace and quiet, which he very rarely got. The long and the short of it was that there wasn't enough money to pay for everything. Instead of risking additional conflict my mum would lie to my dad about the payment of bills, and it was during this that I learnt a valuable skill.

When I was seven years old, during one school holiday we went for a two-week break to a holiday park in North Wales. My mother had booked us all into a self-catering chalet, and she was responsible for all the money and the logistics. My dad was under the impression that she had been saving a monthly sum out of her housekeeping. Unfortunately she had spent most of the money on bills, and we kids could tell she was worried sick.

She had, in fact, only barely saved enough to pay for the journey there. She was on the verge of doing something desperate, and we knew it. It was strange that she would confide in us but not Dad. We always felt responsible for Mum, and we just wanted to protect her, and for all the worry to stop.

During the first evening we came up with a money-making idea. My brothers Andrew and Neville and I were all fairly seasoned locksmiths. We had learnt our trade on the meters back home. That night my mother, or should I say Fagin, gave my unknowing father the remnants of the holiday fund and sent him and his Woodbines off to play bingo. After ten minutes we had Mum's hairgrip and began to pick the electricity meter lock. It was surprising how easy it was. That meter was half full of shillings, and that was a lot more than we got out of the one at home.

Our excitement and the relief on Mum's face were immediate; it was in fact the happiest we had seen her in months. We counted that money twenty times, if not more, and soon decided that it was too lucrative an opportunity to miss.

As anyone who has frequented a holiday park will verify, there are certain times of the day that working class holidaymakers frequent the bingo halls and bars, usually opening time until closing time. We waited until we were sure our adjoining neighbours had gone out for the evening, and then implemented our plan. As I was the runt of the family, it was unanimously decided that I was the only one small enough to fit through the neighbour's tiny chalet kitchen window.

My mum dangled me through by my legs, and I opened the larger window, thus enabling my brother to clamber in. I won't divulge which brother it was because he will kill me. The other brother was too chicken to become a master criminal, so he stayed outside with my mum and my baby sister Ceri.

My brother soon opened the locked meter, and I emptied the near full box into my empty football socks. I was his bag man. Within minutes we had locked up and exited the crime scene. I now knew how the Great Train Robbers must have felt.

In less than an hour we had emptied every meter in our chalet block. We had made a fortune. I had never seen so much money in my entire life, all seven years of it. We spent the following two hours counting all those shillings, and bagging them into one pound amounts. We were rich.

The next stage was not quite as straightforward, as we had to change all the coins into notes. We had to do all that without my father knowing. Again it was soon decided that I would be used to launder the money. I had never been in such high demand. I suddenly became very popular with my brothers.

The following morning my mother woke me early. We caught a bus into Caernarfon, while my father was visiting his family. We went from shop to shop pretending that I was a good little boy who had been saving his hard-earned pocket money. All the shopkeepers were incredibly kind and changed up a pound, or sometimes even two pounds. Some even patted me on the head for being a good lad and gave me free sweets. I didn't feel guilty though, as I didn't know what guilt was then. All I knew was that my mum had been sad, and now we had made her happy.

At the time I didn't realise the seriousness of the escapade, but what was the worst that could have happened to me? I suppose they could have put me in a secure unit, but the chances are I would have escaped to freedom and fled the country. You have to remember that I was now a fully trained master crook.

In adulthood I was unfortunate enough to be in an overseas hotel when an earthquake struck. The hotel staff fled home to their families and left the frightened guests downstairs, cold and alone. I managed to discover the store cupboards and picked the padlocks on all the doors. In no time at all I had distributed hundreds of blankets to the very grateful guests. I even let some of the Germans have bedding. Fortunately for them old habits die hard.

THE RECEPTION AREA—GLAN GWNA HOLIDAY PARK

Meters galore!

Chapter 6

Micky found religion

An inquisitive nature?
Or a nosy sod?
What does it matter?
Micky found God.

As a young child I was forced to go to Catholic church with
Neville and Andrew on a daily basis, as my mother was a strict
Catholic. My maternal grandmother was Jewish, my paternal
grandparents were Baptists, my father a Methodist, and two of
my nieces are Mormons, which left me with no option but to
get confirmed into the Church of England when in adulthood.

The daily church visit meant constant early starts and
plenty of helpings of 'how I would go to hell' if I didn't repent.
I resented this very much. Micky of course took great pleasure
in teasing me for my enforced church attendance. The Church
of England kids had it well sussed, they just attended church
three times a year and held a five-minute assembly every day.

The enforced Christianity, and Micky's daily taunting,
griped an independent, free-thinking kid, so one day I decided
to do something about it.

Now Micky (who thought God was a fish you ate with
chips and peas) was always a curious kid, some say bloody

nosey, so he didn't take much convincing that there was something of spectacular interest within the church.

We decided to set off from Newcroft towards the church on a Saturday morning, with me knowing that Mrs Barry would be cleaning the church, among her other thankless but well-meaning tasks. When we arrived, Micky was fascinated by what he considered to be a gigantic house full of gold and grandeur, so it didn't take long for him to walk towards the altar, towards a hardworking Mrs Barry. I urged him forward, and while he was committing this act of bravery I quietly retreated to the main door. Fortunately Mrs Barry was a trusting soul so had left the keys in the door. This left me no option but to lock the door from the outside, and go home for some dinner.

Many hours later they were released by Father Capper. I believe that to be the first and last time Micky went voluntarily to church. Up until then Father Capper had insisted that I went to church. After this incident we had a mutual understanding: He didn't bother me and I didn't bother him. Again I got a hiding from my mother, but it was well worth it.

Chapter 7

The cream-coloured unicorn

She said, "You can steal from the dead",
"You can spit and curse".
"But God help you",
"If you steal from my purse".

As kids who didn't have a lot, it was incredible how kind we
were to each other. If one of our gang had fags, sweets, pop,
etc., we would always share. I well remember the Christmas of
1970, as Micky received a wonderful present. It was a blue
chipper push bike (small chopper), and for the next three years
he saddle backed me everywhere, which is why he had such big
legs.

It also wasn't unusual for an item of clothing to pass
to another family after it had gone through three siblings
within a family. The comforting thing was that the majority of
us at primary school all wore hand-me-downs, because we all
came from big families.

A couple of years ago my mother came out with a
wonderful quote. She stated "that I was the only child at
primary school who had rugby boots". This was true; however,
she missed out the fact that these were the only footwear I
had. I wore those boots for school and Sunday best. They were

a hand-me-down from my eldest brother Paul, and he was twelve years older than me, and his feet four sizes bigger. To top it off, one of them had a nail sticking through the sole, into my foot. I, therefore, walked around for twelve months with a limp.

It is strange that I remember when people were mean, more so than when they were kind, possibly because people were far more community spirited and kind back then. I found that people who had very little gave more, although, on one Saturday afternoon this was not the case.

It was a hot summer's day, and Micky and I were sitting on the water tank outside his back door. It was too hot to play football, so we decided to melt some ants with a piece of glass and the sun. It wasn't too long before we heard Mr Gallone the ice cream man. The chimes were getting closer, but as usual we were skint. Micky thought for a moment, then leapt off the tank, ran into his kitchen and helped himself to ten pence from his mum's purse. He then bought the biggest ice cream cornet I had ever seen. He sat back on the tank, basking in the sun and licked away at it until his heart was content. Not once did he offer me a lick. I was drooling like a slobbering basset hound.

After a dozen or so licks Micky's mum came out and questioned him on how he came to acquire such a splendid ice cream. As quick as lightning he replied that I had bought it for him. She looked directly into my eyes and asked me if this was true. Now my answer could have gone either way, if he had let me have a lick. I would have lied for him. I told his mum the truth.

She slapped him so hard across the face that I thought his head had spun all the way around, she then snatched the ice cream cornet off him and slammed it into the centre of his forehead. He was so deep in shock that he just sat there with ice cream melting down his face. I remember thinking what a wonderful impression of a unicorn he was doing, but shame about the big ears.

The following day Micky paid me back with interest. He stuffed my pants full of what he told me was cotton wool. It turned out to be fibreglass out of a discarded cooker, so I walked like John Wayne for a week or two.

Chapter 8

Doctors and nurses

"Pass me a scalpel",
"This operation looks tricky".
"Where is the patient"?
"She is underneath Micky".

My introduction into the murky world of sex, and how my friends and I discovered the facts of life, happened on a fine summer afternoon, straight after primary school. Sex was never discussed by adults in our house. I am sure most of us kids just muddled through, picking it up as we went along.

My friends Mark, Dick and Micky and I decided to go digging for treasure underneath one of the old railway arches, alongside the school. While we were there we were disturbed by a girl who was in our class at school. At first we didn't take too much notice of her; however, when she started undressing, our eyes, ears and everything else pricked up.

For the sake of the young lady concerned I will call her Charity (because she was always giving). Mark, Dick and I soon got bored of the fiddling with the very mature Charity, so returned to our gold digging. Micky, however, was doing some strange kind of press up on top of her. (They were very forward at this type of thing, and he still is.) He states that he has to do it three times a day or he gets stomach ache. No wonder his wife always looks tired. The boy was always destined to be on the top shelf.

We must have been making an awful lot of noise because Mrs Jobling, our very strict, Victorian-style teacher, had come out of the school and was standing right behind us. She let out a loud shriek and then frogmarched us all to our homes, telling our parents that we were interfering with innocent Charity. I again got a good hiding, as did Mark and Dick. Micky, the main perpetrator, got a pat on his back and a "that's my boy" from his dad. Who said justice was fair? The topic of sex rarely knowingly reared its ugly head in our house again; however, Charity was always there for practical knowledge.

Unfortunately for me the odd slip-up arose. One chaotic morning at the breakfast table Andrew was absent, so in all innocence I said to my mum that he was probably having a wet dream. This comment was followed by a smack around my head. I honestly thought it meant weeing the bed, and when I discovered what it really meant, I wore two pairs of pants to bed. So, no accidents for me.

Another innocent faux pas regarding sex was again because of a lack of knowledge. I was okay at the practical, but rubbish at the theory. There was an extremely posh, older lad whose parents had just moved into one of the new houses on the private estate. The older kids had nicknamed him Dildo, so I thought that was his name. One morning as he was walking towards the shops with his extremely well-dressed mother, and me being extremely polite shouted across the road at the top of my voice, " 'ello Dildo, going shopping?" The mother looked shocked and shouted, "Who is that horrid little boy?" At the time I thought it was a class thing, but now I know why she was shocked; it just surprises me she knew what a dildo was, as I didn't think Harrods sold them.

Years later we had sex education at school but it was very limited. What the bloody hell do birds and bees have to do with anything? Anyway, Micky always had an excess of porno books to look at during our primary school years. We used to steal them from the builders on the building sites, and then post them through everyone's letter box along West Street. That is if we could get them out of Micky's sweaty palms.

The last time I went underneath those railway arches was in 1975, when I was twelve. I was accompanied by Micky, a lad called Pete and a chirpy Irish lad called Dermot. Our habits were still as disgusting as ever, and we had discovered a new novelty toy, called Durex. We had decided that the best use for them would be to wee into them and tie a knot in the top. Then we stood 10 yards apart and threw them to each other: a vagabond version of pass the parcel. By coincidence the urine-filled condom would always burst while in mid flight towards poor Dermot. Because of this vulgar game and constant bad luck he always stank of urine, and dogs would follow him for miles. He was the pied piper of Weedon.

Sadly, while writing this book, I was informed that Dermot had taken his own life in a lonely bed-sit. He was such an honourable person. He left his rent money for the landlord, by his bed.

A tunnel of love.

Another tunnel of love.

Chapter 9

General Patton

I wanted to play football,
And score lots of goals.
Not dress like a girl guide,
With clothes full of holes.

What should have been a major event in my childhood turned
out to be a memorable disaster. As I have mentioned before,
all the kids in our street wore hand-me-downs, but if you went
outside your street into another area, second-hand clothing was
not always seen. I had not known I was at a disadvantage until
I joined the Cub Scouts.

Because I was such a short lad, my shorts were nearly
long trousers, and my tatty Cub jumper was like a long dress
that was three times too big. My jumper had originally been
worn by my brothers: Paul in 1957, Neville in 1965 and
Andrew in 1968. I then inherited it in 1970. I hadn't realised
that the Cubs had more rules than the Masons. I only joined so
I could play in their stupid five-a-side football team.

I nervously attended my first meeting, not knowing
that I should not be wearing all the medals and badges that
were adorning my jumper. I was more highly decorated than
General Patton. I wore all the badges that my brothers had

earned and some more that my mother had sewn on for good measure.

During the evening a very gentle lady called Akele took me aside and explained that I would have to remove all my badges by the following week, because I hadn't earned them. What was my mother trying to do to me? Even at that early age I wondered why all the Royals were allowed to wear all their medals, so why not me? Anyway, with all that regalia I probably out ranked most of them.

I soon realised why my mother had left all the badges on the jumper, it was to cover up all the moth holes. The following week I arrived at the Cub hut, along with my fellow Cubs, who were crying with laughter at my original attire. All the holes were uncovered, and I was in full view of them all. I was nicknamed Moth Boy, and to finish off the fiasco, I was issued with a brown woggle, because there were no more white ones. Moth Boy was the only Cub with a brown woggle, so he resigned quietly. Who knows, I could have been a Sixer by now.

There were children with a lot less than me, though. One little lad called Geoff springs to mind. He was small, with a square head and ginger hair. We used to say, "Geoff's square-shaped head shows how a good head should be", a play on the Chefs square-shaped soup advert.

Along with his mum, dad, brother and sister, he moved to Weedon from the Welsh valleys. He was one of the most naturally gifted footballers that I had ever seen, as he had pace and skill. He loved Leeds United, and was forever thinking that he was Peter Lorimer (Leeds player of the 1970s). Whenever he played, he used to give a radio commentary, and whenever he passed you with the ball he pretended he was changing gear. I could never tackle him because I was too busy listening to his commentary or laughing. Now, looking back, I realise that he probably had Tourette's syndrome.

On many occasions I watched Geoff playing with the younger lads and thought with the right coaching and a lot of luck he could have gone places. Unfortunately little Geoff's dad died when we were at primary school and his poor old mum struggled to bring up the three kids.

Sometimes in life people only get the breaks because of family connections and money. Geoff never got any. He could never join the Cubs, because he didn't have a uniform, and he could never develop his football as he didn't have any kit. People only let you play in a team if you have the right gear.

Geoff still lives at home, works all the hours god sends and looks after his partially disabled brother. Life was destined to be hard for him.

Chapter 10

School pantomimes

I could have been an actor,
Even though I'm not gay.
I was born to play Joseph,
However not in their play.

At the ripe old age of eight, I entered the class of Mr Davies. He was the strictest teacher I had ever met. He thought nothing of hitting his pupils in the centre of their backs, or rapping us on the top of our heads with his knuckles. He favoured me a little because he, like my father was Welsh speaking. They were both from the old school that said children should be seen and not heard. I knew he had a soft spot for me because he didn't hit me as much as some of the other boys. Mr Davies had a wonderful catch phrase: Just before he clouted us he would shout "Rat-a-tat-tat, soft and silly boy", and then whack. The strange thing was that we all quite liked him.

We used to wait impatiently for the pantomime season to start, to see who would get the part of Joseph and play opposite the lovely Suzie. All the boys fancied her, and her mum and dad had a pub. She was the perfect woman, or at least the perfect eight-year-old girl.

Much to my dismay Mr Davies gave me the scabby old role of being the first innkeeper. I was devastated, as I was born to play Joseph. My mate Alan Farmer was to play Joseph. Geoff's square-shaped head was to be a donkey. Others played minor roles, and I ended up a bloody innkeeper. I went into the king of all sulks.

Rehearsals went to plan and the big night arrived. The wonderful nativity story began in the usual fashion: there was a star in the sky, and an angel appeared, blah, blah, blah. Eventually Joseph, the delectable Suzie, I mean Mary, and Geoff the donkey knocked on my door (it made a change from bailiffs), and they requested a room for the night. I was supposed to say, "I am sorry there is no room at the inn", but instead, being very jealous, blurted out that "there is plenty of room upstairs mate, please come in".

For what seemed an eternity the room went silent, then they totally ignored me and went clip-clopping off towards the next inn. I remember thinking that it comes to something when a donkey with cardboard ears ignores me. Mr Davies gave me the benefit of the doubt and put it down to an outburst of stage fright, and he made me the leading man in his following production.

Mr Davies decided to break with tradition and wrote a play of his own. It was about a dopey little boy who hadn't got a Christmas tree. The final scene had me as a little boy and Karen Gargan dressed as a little Christmas tree. I was to gently cart that little tree off the stage and then enjoy the rapturous applause from my adoring audience. That time, however, I really did get stage fright and froze solid. As a result, the little tree carted the dopey little boy off the stage. I felt it added a fine twist to the tale. Mr Davies did not see it that way, and I was never asked to star again.

The following year Mr Davies retired home to Wales, to look after his mother. We took up a collection and bought him a spade; all of us put in money. When he said goodbye I, along with others, began to cry. He was as hard as nails but fair. We respected and liked him and we believed he liked us.

My lovely old primary school. Sadly, now demolished and houses have replaced it.

Class photograph: I am in the front row, fourth from right. Micky is sixth from the left, middle row. Joseph, Mary and Karen the Christmas tree are all in there.

Another view of the beautiful school.

Chapter 11

Fields of dreams

Not a care in the world,
As long as we were fed.
There is nowt as funny,
As a boy stuck by his head.

When we lived at 8 Newcroft, life should have been so wonderful and so simple. The summers were hotter, the snows were deeper, and people used to get by without any money. The majority of people in our park had large families, so our childhood gang consisted of kids whose ages ranged from four to fourteen. Older ones would watch over the younger ones.

We used to walk for miles playing cowboys and Indians, Romans and Britons, British and Germans and many, many more. We built forts and camps and weapons of all descriptions. We made catapults, bows and arrows and bombs. It was amazing that no one was killed, and to my knowledge only two kids I knew lost an eye. I soon got fed up playing Romans and Britons though, because everyone apart from me would be a Roman, and they would chase me for miles and whack me with sticks.

We walked for hours to find the biggest conkers, or bullheads and minnows, or a regular favourite would be river jumping. Another special place was the old burnt-out thatched farm house on West Street, where I fell off the roof and broke my leg. I bounced like a space hopper. My tip to anyone who tries to jump from one building to another building, twenty feet in the air, is don't jump in rugby boots.

One afternoon we walked for miles following a very low-flying hot-air balloon, and on the way back home we tried to take a shortcut across a field full of bullocks. The older boys easily managed to cross the field at pace, without drawing too much attention from the curious bullocks. This left a handful of us younger lads stranded behind. Our protectors had left us again. The older ones jeered and teased us, and as usual we were talked into crossing, even though we were petrified of the giant beasts.

When we had plucked up enough courage we ran at top speed across the uneven field, straight through all the cow pats. The adrenaline rush was awesome. Unfortunately for us, the jeering and whooping had enticed the bullocks towards us, and they were getting nearer and nearer.

At the edge of the field I just managed to dive underneath the barbed wire, commando style, whereas some of the more agile kids dived over the top. We all landed in the stinging nettles, but it was better than being bitten to death by a man-eating bullock.

We had travelled so fast that we forgot to make sure Bab (Boo Boo) was safe. Bab was the youngest of the Watts children, and they lived opposite us at 8 Newcroft. He was called Bab because he was barely more than a baby, but his real name was Simon. Mr and Mrs Watts thought it would be easier if all the children and pets had names beginning with the letter S: Stephen, Sharon, Stuart, Shaun, Simon, Sheena the dog, Sherry the cat and Smokey the rabbit.

Because Bab was the baby of our group, we were supposed to protect him. When we turned around, at what we considered to be a safe area, we saw that he was hanging from the barbed wire by the seat of his pants. He resembled a German paratrooper hanging from a tree. The bullocks loved the screaming, poo-smelling Bab so much that they began nudging, sniffing and licking him, so we left him dangling for half an hour until the bullocks got fed up of his crying and wandered off. Ironically, we didn't give a sod about his safety, we were too busy dancing about and singing, "They're coming to take you away Boo Boo".

We eventually managed to stop him crying, and buy his silence with a bag of sweets. Thankfully he didn't tell his parents or we would have all been for the high jump. Secretly we all enjoyed his wailings, because it was one the many days he ended up bawling.

Not all our exploits were as enjoyable. On the odd occasion we used to hang around with some kids from the top end of the village, and often we would wander up to the main road (Watling Street), outside the Crossroads Hotel. Here we watched the cars and motorbikes go past. On one wet Saturday afternoon we witnessed an elderly gentleman and his wife drive a car out of the hotel car park, straight onto the busy main road. There was a loud screech of brakes and an almighty noise. An articulated lorry had somehow collided with the car, and had removed the roof off the car.

We were terribly nosey so ran to the crash site. We looked into the wreckage and to our horror we saw the elderly gentleman's head on the back seat of his car, while his body was still in the front. His tiny wife was just staring ahead, shaking, in shock, but otherwise unscathed. I couldn't understand why she wasn't crying or screaming and also why there was so little blood.

The local policeman eventually turned up and moved us along. I was left feeling that I had committed a crime, like I was bad. We never told anyone what we had seen and we never discussed it again. The only time I think about it is when I am asleep.

One of my better days was during the summer in the early 1970s. It was a beautiful day and the sun was baking hot, so we all decided to go river jumping down lovers' lane. We knew that the older bigger boys could jump farther than we could; however, the rule was if one attempted a jump the rest had to follow. Most of the time, I just jumped straight in the water. Because my legs were so short, I knew I would get soaked. I thought at least that way I wouldn't hurt myself. I would get a slap for being wet and dirty, anyway.

One of the lads was nicknamed Alien because his mum always cut his hair the same shape as a space helmet. He was a sporty athletic type, who was very good at long jumping. He was a very confident river jumper, so much so that he attempted the biggest jump of all, in an area where even the older lads wouldn't try, to earn our respect.

He sized up the distance and paced out his run up, turned around and looked every bit a champion, then hurled himself at full pelt towards the edge of the bank. None of us knew that there was some rusty old wire at foot height in the long grass at the edge, and he tripped over it and plunged head first into the filthy river.

The next thirty seconds seemed like minutes. His head was stuck in years of cow muck and sludge on the bed of the river, leaving just his legs wriggling in mid air. Not one of us went to his aid, we were laughing too much. When he managed to break free and stood upright, his body was totally encased in muck with only the whites of his eyes showing. He looked like a character from a blackface minstrel. This was one of the funniest moments in my life, and was the only time that I wet myself because of excessive laughter. We laughed even more at the prospect of him drowning.

I often look back at that period with great joy and a certain amount of sadness, as two of the older lads are no longer with us. Steve passed away in a tragic bike accident during his late teens and Wally died in an electrical accident. Both those lads were honourable, hard-working, salt-of-the-earth boys, and their deaths were a great loss to their family, friends and the estate.

During another one of our expeditions, a very strange thing happened to me. Like most other children before us and after us, we were told never to play on the railway line. We of course knew better. We would walk across the fields towards Stowe-Nine-Churches, which was an incredibly small village, without shops or even a pub. As children we could only find three interesting facts about Stowe: one was its name, and the other two were that trains had crashed there in 1915 and 1951, killing quite a few people.

It all began one sunny afternoon in 1973 during the school holidays, when a handful of the other kids and I yomped the three miles up to the Stowe railway tunnel. We decided that it would be a good idea to enter the dark tunnel and walk along the track. We were all terrified, but the buzz was incredible. We scuttled along the track keeping totally quiet until we were half way through, when we then felt the rumble of a train. We couldn't run back as it was too far and we couldn't outrun the train going forwards. We were absolutely petrified. The buzz had now gone and screams took over. Dermot decided we would have to get into one of the recesses and press ourselves firmly against the wall. We had been told by adults on numerous occasions that if you stood too close to a train you could be pulled underneath, so that theory was to be put to the test.

The train approached at an incredible speed, and the noise was horrendous, which fortunately drowned out my girlie screams. For what seemed like an eternity the train flew past, quickly followed out of the dark tunnel by half a dozen yelping kids. It was an experience I was never to repeat.

The last thing that my mother had said when I left the house that morning was behave yourself, keep away from the canal, keep away from the railway line, don't smoke, don't swear and be home for your tea at 5:30 sharp. I had let her down on the first five requests, so I felt it was only right to obey her on the time keeping. You see at that point in my young life I had not perfected the art of lying, and she could see straight through me.

I did not have a watch, but I knew it was about 3:00 P.M., as I had checked the time with two of the lads. I decided to walk home alone, and I had left myself plenty of time. The last thing I recall is hurling crab apples from the end of a stick at the remaining boys and yelling a few swear words at them. It had been an exciting day, and I felt good.

I eventually walked through our front door at 8:00 P.M., to a very angry and worried mother. She had been told by the other lads of the time I left them, and exactly where I had been playing, so I again was to join the sore arse brigade. I could not explain where the missing five hours went, and still can't. I had left the lads at the railway line, and the next thing I remembered was exiting a field by the council garages at the bottom of Newcroft. It is to be one of my life's mysteries, as I was not distressed in any way.

Stowe tunnel

This is where we watched the cars go by.

Watling Street, the old Roman road.

Weedon, looking to Stores

Part of the river that we jumped.

The Round Hill. My favourite place to play.

L. & N.W.R. MANCHESTER EXPRESS NEAR WEEDON.   318.
By The Locomotive Publishing Company, Ltd., London.

A train just outside Weedon.

Chapter 12

1974

They said it would be lonely that Christmas,
Without you to hold.
But it's lonely forever,
Lonely and cold.

Without any comparison 1974 was the most memorable year of my life. We moved from the estate into the large government depot, where my father worked as a storekeeper. It was one of the largest government stores in the country, supplying the military, post offices, prisons, embassies, etc., with all government-issue household appliances. The move took place the same month I started at my senior education, at Bugbrooke Campion Comprehensive School, five miles away. It might as well have been on the other side of the world.

I left primary school on an educational high, as I had been given the most gold stars issued to any of the boys in my class. Unfortunately I never got a chance to sit the Eleven Plus. I assumed it was because we couldn't afford all the posh grammar school gear.

I hadn't even been at Bugbrooke a week, when I was sent to the staff corridor by some disgruntled teacher, for committing a minor offence. This was not the new creepy start

I was hoping for. I had committed the heinous crime of walking around with soaking wet hair and shirt. I wasn't even given a chance to protest my innocence, or make up a worthwhile excuse. I could hardly tell the teacher that I had been bog washed by fourth-year girls, who proceeded to get my little willy out and have a fiddle. Grassing was never an acceptable option for me.

On 14 October 1974 at 3:00 P.M., I was summoned from my maths lesson and ordered again to the dreaded staff corridor, I couldn't understand why, or what for. I took every precaution and hid my ten No 6 cigarettes down my pants. It is strange what you remember from major times in your life, but I know there were ten in the packet because I hadn't undone the seal, and I owed Alien one from that morning's school bus journey. I also remember thinking that I should really give up smoking, perhaps after *that* packet. I was eleven years old.

When I arrived at the staff corridor, Neville, who was fifteen, and Andrew, who was thirteen, were angrily waiting for me. Their exact words were, "You fat pig, what have you been up to? You wait until we get you home". To be honest I wasn't sure if I had done something or not, because I was always in mischief, but we were soon to find out.

Mr Roberts, the Headmaster, called us into his office. He was a large Yorkshire man who had served in the Desert

Rats during the war. We knew better than to mess with him. Miss Rodgers was the Deputy Headmaster, and she was sitting to his left looking extremely sad. I remember thinking, "What's up with you, lost your purse or something?". Mr Roberts uttered some words, and they will stay with me forever. He said, "Sit down, lads, I have some very bad news for you. I am very sorry to inform you that your elder sister Gwyneth has died".

My whole world collapsed within two sentences. We all broke down into floods of tears, and Mr Roberts took us home to the depot in his Land Rover. I must have gone into shock, because I thought that he had said she had been stabbed to death. I soon found out that Gwyn had taken an overdose of aspirins.

I cannot write down how that pain felt or still feels now. It was worse than any break or beating. My stomach hurt so much, and I felt so empty, as if a part of my soul had been ripped out and was now gone forever. I hurt like I never hurt before, or I hope I never hurt again.

At age eleven I didn't understand religion. I just thought that I would never see my darling Gwyn again, the person I most loved in the world. She was my big sister, and we had a special bond. I used to dance around on her feet; she taught me to read; she showed me more love and affection than anyone ever had. When she had first left home at age sixteen, Micky and I had walked three miles to see her in her new home. We were only five.

In the past Gwyn had always been there to protect and comfort me, but during the time after her death there was no-one. I discovered that adults don't know what to say to kids when they are grieving. They know how to comfort adults, but not kids.

Gwyn was buried in the graveyard with my Granddad, the graveyard where I had previously visited. Gwyn's little boy David soon came to live with us, after a short stay with some kind neighbours, Seamus and Yvonne. He was made a ward of the court. Even though he was our nephew we raised him as our brother.

After a week of mourning I returned to school. It was an incredibly difficult journey, and life would never be the same again. I remember clearly thinking that the only thing that we are certain of is death, and figured out that it is how and when people die that affects us the most. I realised we just had to get on with life, like everybody else.

As a child I was envious of our neighbours five miles away, the Spencer's at Althorp. They had a big house, gardens and lots of money, and I honestly believed that they were worry free. It wasn't until I reached adulthood that I realised that wealth doesn't buy you a pain-free life. When poor Princess Di passed away many people mourned, and likewise with my Gwyn, the only difference was the size of the funeral. The pain was the same.

Sadly, whenever I dream of Gwyn I picture her lying in her shroud, after the post mortem, and I can never get that picture out of my head. Now when I grieve, I grieve for my Gwyn, and I grieve for myself as a child. I seem to be on the outside looking down at myself from above.

A song that I heard in later life reminds me of that moment: Alison Moyet singing "This House". I find it strange, but that song seems to fit how I felt perfectly. I pray that there is a heaven because I know Gwyn will be there, waiting for me, (that is if I get there).

This is the place where we moved.

The road Micky and I walked up to see Gwyn when she first got married.

Gwyn aged 16.

Gwyn protecting me as usual.

Neville with a basin haircut and Andrew in a girl's bathing costume.

Gwyn and David (top). Gwyn, David and Ceri (bottom)

Gwyn and little David.

My brother Paul is on the right, Gwyn to his left, Neville to her left, Andrew to his right, and me smiling. We stood by someone else's car to look posh.

Chapter 13

Life at Bugbrooke

They taught me maths,
They taught me to spell.
Five years of torture,
Half a decade of hell.

I would like to say, "Kids are okay, I used to go to school with them", however this was not the case when I went back to school after Gwyn's death. The kids had been told about her death, and about how she had died, but they still wanted to know all the gory details. I didn't know the details and still don't.

Being at school was horrendous. Some of the kids were very cruel, few were sensitive, and I found that ordeal extremely hard to cope with. The situation finally came to a head when my class was shown a film of a dead drug addict's post mortem. This was meant to deter us from taking drugs, but it just reminded me of what my poor sister Gwyn went through. I returned home that evening and faked an injured ankle. Eventually the hospital plastered my leg and I stayed off school for months.

When I returned to school things started to improve. I began peaking again in my merits (see certificates), and I was in the top flight. Our class had won the cricket championship. I was captain of our class football team, and I represented the school at football and Rugby Union. I even started to enjoy going to school.

It was about that time that a couple of my classmates told me that when their primary school played against my primary school at football, they were afraid to tackle me because they thought I was disabled. They went on to say that they thought I was a Thalidomide child because I had little legs, squat body, big nose and a bloody great head. What did they expect from a boy who had a maternal Jewish grandmother and a Welsh father, a 6-foot, pug-nosed Adonis? Cheeky sods. I personally think they were just jealous of my fancy footwork. I am pleased to report that my body is now as fat as my head, and my nose has been smashed into reduction.

As usual in life, I thought everything was going fine, and then bang, more hell on earth. One Saturday evening Mum, little David and Ceri had been to see the black-and-white minstrel show at the local village hall. Neville and Andrew were out with their mates and I was out with Micky. My dad was at home with his FM radio, his cups of tea and his Woodbines. Nightly he would sit in his chair for hours, listening to the police channel, puffing away.

That night I met my mother at the main depot gates at

10:00 P.M. We only had one set of keys so had to enter and exit at the same times, which was a real pain. In future months we used to hide the key underneath a stone outside the gate, without my father's knowledge, as he was a stickler for rules and regulations.

When we entered the gates we noticed that my dad was walking down the yard towards us, looking very distressed. He had been listening to the radio and had heard numerous police messages referring to a serious motorcycle accident, five miles away, just outside the Althorp estate. He had heard that a young male was seriously injured, and the parents should be informed straight away. Dad had a sixth sense and knew it was one of us, even though we were banned from going on motorbikes.

He was right, as the telephone rang and he was told to go to the Northampton General Hospital right away, as Neville was in intensive care. He had been a pillion passenger on a motorbike, got knocked off by a van and then run over by a friend on another bike. He was dragged underneath the bike, badly smashed up and a major artery ripped out. He was in a bad way.

My mother was rushed to the hospital and taken straight to intensive care, as the doctors were unsure whether Neville would live or die. My mother sat by his bed and a priest gave him the last rites. We all prayed that night.

Neville fought for days to stay alive, then he fought for weeks to keep his leg, and then he fought for many months to get out of his wheelchair and walk again. He was in hospital for a year, and mum was by his side every afternoon and evening.

As children we were taught to hide our emotions, so we couldn't tell Neville how much we were hurting for him. It was during Neville's long stay in hospital that I had to grow up, and we all became very protective of Neville. When eventually Neville went out to the pub on his crutches, a much smaller, younger me was sent to drag him home. He was paralytic, as everyone in the pub had bought him a drink, and he couldn't stand up.

Again when I returned to school, the vultures were waiting to know all the gory details. Good news travels fast; however, bad news travels faster.

Name: *Chris Griffiths*   **Form:** *M2 CB*

You have obtained this certificate by gaining an 'A' for your efforts in four or more of the school subjects as shown below:

MATHS	HISTORY	ART
ENGLISH	FRENCH	MUSIC
SCIENCE *PHYSICS* *BIOLOGY*	R.E B	WOODWORK B
GEOGRAPHY B	P.E.	NEEDLEWORK

Date *November '75*   Form Tutor. *Barr*

A good all-round effort

Head of House. *J. A. Cooper*

MERIT

Name: *Christopher Griffiths*   **Form:** *M2 CB*

You have obtained this certificate by gaining an 'A' for your efforts in four or more of the school subjects as shown below

MATHS	HISTORY	ART
ENGLISH	FRENCH	MUSIC
A· SCIENCE	R.E	WOODWORK
GEOGRAPHY	P.E	NEEDLEWORK
		BIOLOGY

Well done, Chris! A good start for the year.

Date. *October 1975*   Form Tutor. *Dan*

Very good.

Head of House. *J. A. Cooper*

Name: *Christopher Griffiths*   **Form:** *M1CB*

You have obtained this certificate by gaining an 'A' for your efforts in four or more of the school subjects as shown below:

MATHS	HISTORY	ART CRAFT & DESIGN
ENGLISH	FRENCH	MUSIC
SCIENCE	R.E.	WOODWORK /METALWORK
GEOGRAPHY	P.E.	NEEDLEWORK /HOUSECRAFT

Congratulations, Chris! You've managed to sweep the board this time, all 'A's.

Date. *March '75*   Form Tutor. _____

Head of House. *J. A. Cooper*

MERIT

Name: _Chris Griffiths_   **Form:** _M2CB_

You have obtained this certificate by gaining an 'A' for your efforts in four or more of the school subjects as shown below:

MATHS	HISTORY	ART
ENGLISH	FRENCH	MUSIC
SCIENCE	R.E.	WOODWORK
GEOGRAPHY	P.E.	NEEDLEWORK
BIOLOGY		

Even illness can't hold you down!

Date _February '76_   **Form Tutor.** _Ben_

Head of House. _J.A. Cooper_

CAMPION SCHOOL

MERIT

Name: _Chris Griffiths_   Form: _M2CB_

You have obtained this certificate by gaining an 'A' for your efforts in four or more of the school subjects as shown below.

MATHS   · HISTORY   ART

ENGLISH   FRENCH   MUSIC

SCIENCE   R.E   WOODWORK

GEOGRAPHY   P. E.   NEEDLEWORK

Date. _April '76_   Form Tutor. _____

Head of House. _J. A. Cooper_

Chapter 14

Batman's birthday

People are generous,
In the year of the rat.
But food was a plenty,
In the year of the bat.

When I entered my early teens I discovered that my world was expanding. I started hanging around with kids who lived on other estates and even some who came from other villages.

One day in particular, Micky and I were playing football in the main playing field with some lads from the lower end of the village. There was Danny, Adie, Dave and Batman, and it was in fact Batman's birthday.

Batman was a good lad. He was one of four children, and his dad was a decent bloke, a German who had been captured during the Second World War. This of course meant little to us, because all our dads and granddads had been servicemen. It didn't really matter to us whose side anyone was on, because they were all brave, and anyway Batman was always generous with his fags. We called him Batman because he thought he could fly, and he looked like a bat. As usual none of us had any money and none of us wanted to go home for food, as we would be kept in for one reason or another.

At the bottom of the playing field was the village hall with an adjoining annexe, and this was often used for parties and meetings. We noticed a large number of cars outside and a lot of activity, so we felt compelled to investigate. Where there were people there was a good chance of scrounging fags, or maybe even a beer between us.

When we got to the exterior of the annexe we realised that the windows on each side were wide open, to let the warm summer breeze waft through, and we also noticed that it was a big, flashy wedding and that there was lots of grub lying about. The tables in the annexe were stacked with every type of food you could dream of: sandwiches, crisps, cakes, fruit, nuts, cheeses and loads of things that I had never even seen before. And to top it off there was wine, lovely wine.

I was quite happy just to look and drool, but Micky had other ideas. We soon established that all these well-dressed, posh people were busy giving speeches and patting each other on the back. The opportunity was too big to miss. Micky (who I am sure was Huckleberry Finn in a previous life) decided that we should hold our own party to celebrate Batman's birthday, and we should borrow some of the wonderful-looking wedding food from the annexe. It was agreed that we would drop Micky through one of the open windows, and he would run past the open hall door, swipe an item, then run to the other open window, where two of us would pull him out.

We dropped him through the window, and like a well-trained soldier he picked up two bottles of Champagne and ran to the other window, where he was successfully pulled out. I remember thinking, "What a pro". Danny was next to be dropped behind enemy lines. He collected a plate of sandwiches. Aidy went next and got a basket of fruit. That was quite a novel choice because the only time we ever ate fruit was when we were ill, or if we had been scrumping. Dave was the next to go, and heroically came back with nuts and crisps, and then birthday boy Batman completed his mission with two bottles of wine. We were going to have the feast of all feasts.

Unfortunately my excitement was short lived, as my friends noted that one of us had not been in, and that was me. I insisted that we had already plenty of luxuries, and we didn't need any more. I was reminded of the unwritten rule of "if one person does something the rest have to follow suit", and ironically I was more frightened of being called a coward.

I was petrified, because I knew if I was caught stealing I would get a well-deserved hiding from my mother. At risk of being the village chicken I was dropped through the window, and I froze solid. The lads cheered me on, telling me what items to take. They all told me to take different things, so I got more and more confused and was stuck to the spot. It was like a bad dream, especially as I could hear the clapping in the adjoining hall, and the speeches had come to an end. The guests were as far as the door when I unfroze, and I clearly heard Micky say, "Get the cake". He later said he meant the small chocolate one.

I remember rushing at full speed towards the three-tiered wedding cake and scooping the underneath of the bottom tier with my hands. I didn't want to be accused of stealing the lovely cake stand. The guests started to run towards me; they were only a few feet away, so I threw the massive cake towards the open window where Micky was standing. The top tier hit him square in the face, and the second and third tier hit the window frame and went everywhere. It was like an exploding bomb. I jumped like an athlete straight after it.

And to my amazement the brave lads grabbed me by the arms, and pulled me ninety percent of the way through the window, but not before one of the well-oiled guests had grabbed my feet. They were now playing tug-of-war, with me as the rope. Fortunately for me the guest's hands slipped off my sweaty feet and he flew back into the well-stocked food tables, with one of my plimsolls in his hand. He lay in the remnants of the cake with all the other food on top of him. We ran for miles, screeching and whooping like red Indians after a successful cattle raid.

Occasionally when this episode gets discussed, I am always made to feel guilty (so much so that I never attend weddings, and I got married in a registry office with two witnesses). I would like to say to the bride and groom that I sincerely apologise, and would like to pay for all the food, and please can I have my black, size three plimsoll back? No matter what changes took place in my life, I could always picture us eating like lords and celebrating Batman's birthday.

There weren't many luxuries when we were children, but we always tried to have a laugh, unfortunately sometimes at the expense of someone else's misery. I often wondered how we would all turn out. None of us could foresee that one day Danny would end his life on a railway line.

THE BARRACKS, WEEDON.

The pub where Danny lived.

The exact spot where Danny and I went fishing; we shared my sandwiches and his fags. I have never fished since.

Chapter 15

Father Christmas

Father Christmas is coming,
I can hear the deer canter.
Hold on to your rodents,
It's the foul-mouthed old Santa.

Many of the naughty things we did as children were due to boredom; however, I make no excuses. I know that the majority of children managed to keep out of mischief; unfortunately I wasn't one of them. Now, as an adult, it gives me great pleasure to donate money to the Rotary Club, Round Table and the Freemasons, as they do a wonderful job and help many less fortunate people.

Christmas was a very sad time for my mother and father when I was a baby. My father was ill, and there was no money for presents, decorations and food. It must have been an extremely distressing time for my parents. We kids didn't always realise the seriousness of situations. We were pretty resilient, but Mum and Dad had to do all the worrying. My parents were of a generation where if you didn't work, you didn't eat. They didn't know how claim all the benefits; there weren't all the benefit awareness adverts then. They just did their best, and were very proud people.

I was too young to remember one situation in particular, but my brothers tell me that on a certain Christmas the Round Table delivered presents and a food hamper to our home. I wish I had been more aware as I would have asked for a great big train set.

Years after that event, my friends Dick and Mark (see "Doctors and nurses" chapter) and I, were following the Round Table's Santa Sleigh around the village. It was a wonderful sight. Even though we were in our early teens and we didn't believe in Father Christmas, we still treated it as a mystical time. I so looked forward to Christmas Day, because it was the only day that my mother and father did not argue.

We followed old Santa's sleigh, which was timber, festively painted, with lights on it, speakers blaring out Christmas carols and plonked on top of a low flatbed lorry. Santa's dopey reindeers were also made of wood, but they resembled donkeys.

After following the sleigh for miles, we were totally worn out, so thought that there would be no harm in sitting on the rear of the lorry, with our legs hanging off the back. We considered it to be harmless; we could have always doubled as his elves. We sat there about five minutes, having a wonderful time waving to everyone. I knew how the Queen must have felt, and I enjoyed my brief moment in the public eye. Obviously Santa's big nose must have been put out of joint by the attention we were receiving, because his exact words to us were, "Piss off, the back of the lorry is not for kids".

Now if he had asked us politely we would have reacted in a totally different way, however this was a red rag to a bull. We were used to that approach from adults, so we knew how to handle him, and anyway, our feelings were hurt.

We wandered ahead of the not-so-jolly Santa and his cronies, and travelled down West Street, until we were alongside the old burnt-out farmhouse. It was then that we saw the biggest rat in the world; it was massive. Without any words spoken, Dick ran after it like a Jack Russell and pounced. His right Doc Marten boot went right up the backside of the poor rodent, and it flew through the air like a rugby ball. Johnny Wilkinson would have been proud. The flying rat hit a brick wall, in between two upstairs windows of a house. We were lucky it didn't go straight through one of them. It then slid down the wall, dead. We soon decided that the poor thing should not have died in vain, so I put the rat in my parka pocket.

Minutes later the waving Santa and his glittering entourage drew up level with us, and we put our plan into action. We again sat on the back of the lorry and waited. Old misery guts Santa was then at boiling point, and reacted as expected. His exact words were, "I won't tell you again. F*** off before you get my toe up your a***". Well, I know what present Santa Claus got that year. Like a gunslinger I drew the rat out of my pocket and threw it onto Santa's lap, and he screamed like a big woman. He jumped out of his sleigh, off the back of the lorry and chased us, hurling obscenities.

There was no way on earth that an overweight, overdressed, middle-aged Father Christmas was ever going to catch us. I remember thinking that he would never deliver all his presents before Christmas, if he moved at that speed.

Chapter 16

The counsellor's corset

A middle-aged woman,
With an ample bust.
Schoolboys spying,
With a teen-age lust.

One of the oldest streets in Weedon was West Street.
Originally there were about forty houses, and then in the 1970s
dozens more were added. At one end of the street, opposite
the Plume of Feathers pub was a small Victorian house
occupied by a lady of older years, called Mrs Cicely Blackwell
(Mrs B).

One morning on a cold, wet miserable day Micky and
I knocked on her door, requesting any casual weekend jobs.
We used to knock on everyone's door. She felt sorry for us
wet, ratty little vagabonds and gave us a hot cup of tea, which
was the beginning of an unusual lifetime friendship.

One of the first jobs Mrs B gave us was to bury a dead
mouse that her cat had killed. I carefully dug the hole in her
flower bed and waited for pallbearer Micky to pass me the
mouse. Because he had a very short attention span, he had
thrown the mouse over the wall. It took us ten years to confess
that to Mrs B.

We soon realised that Mrs B was a kind, honest, trusting and wonderful lady, who loved and trusted animals and humans alike. She became a dear friend to us and was the most major influence in our lives. People often commented on why a more than sixty-year-old woman would befriend two little sods. The answer was that she cared. It didn't seem at all unusual to us, she was just another great friend.

She allowed Micky and I to frequent her house as often as we wished, and she was very liberal. She let us smoke and cuss, and didn't judge us too harshly. Mrs B helped me develop a spiritual side to my nature. Unfortunately, I seem to feel everybody's pain.

Over the next fifteen years we were often in her company, she even took us on holiday to South Wales. And when Micky and I brought sand into the holiday place and were chastised, she stood by us, and took us home. If we had not met Mrs B we would have probably ended up in a remand school. We would most certainly have ended up in far more trouble than we did. Everybody should be lucky enough to have a Mrs B in their lives; she was heaven sent to us.

Obviously, I was a little bleeder, who pushed everyone to the limit, including a very patient Mrs B; however, she could dish it out if she needed to. One cold, frosty Saturday morning Micky and I rang her doorbell for what seemed like an eternity.

She eventually came to the door, and sent us into the kitchen to make ourselves a cup of tea. She was busy altering and measuring a dress for a local councillor, who was undressing upstairs. Mrs B would often take in sewing for a few extra quid, to try and make ends meet. As I said before, people didn't know how to get the benefits then.

We were typical boys and were extremely inquisitive, and the thought of a partially clad woman upstairs was too much for us to ignore. We quietly crept up the stairs, and in one of the rooms we could see a reflection in the full-length mirror of a middle-aged, attractive, middle-class woman, who was dressed in just a corset. It was just too good to miss, so we crept up a little farther, to the top of the stairs, so we could get a better eyeful.

Mrs B was a canny old bird, and had a good idea of what we were up to, so she closed the bedroom door. We were devastated; our periscopes were up. Mrs B had, however, overlooked one snag. The bedroom doors could be locked from the outside. She had hurt our feelings, so we would hurt hers. We locked them both in the bedroom. I am sure I should have been a prison officer, as I have always had a fascination with locking doors. After five minutes of banging and shouting we decided that she had been punished enough, so I let her out.

For the very first time she surprised me. She slapped me, then Micky full force around the face, and then around the legs. Micky and I made a hasty retreat to the lounge, momentarily stunned. We didn't talk to each other for at least two minutes, and that was an all-time record. Then Micky had a cunning plan. He decided that it would be a good idea to punch me full force in the leg, causing it to bruise, and to cut my face with a sharp implement that he had found in Mrs B's sewing box. He said that this wonderful idea would convince Mrs B that she had committed a terrible atrocity, and then she would cook us some chips. And if that failed we could threaten to sue her for damages. I was a very unwilling guinea pig but thought the suffering would be worth it.

After a lot of fumbling and pain we managed to produce enough bruising and blood to convince the most cynical of juries. I was marched, limping through the adjoining room, dripping blood with a dead leg, swiftly followed by my legal representative, the honourable Sir Micky. His opening charge of cruelty to minors was swiftly halted by Mrs B. Her response was, "Bleed to death you little b******, and p*** off". It didn't seem quite right coming out of the mouth of a respectable older lady. After this incident we respected her more, and tried not to overstep the mark again; well, not often anyway.

Mrs B was a wonderful person, who is always in my thoughts. She gave us a chance when no-one else would. A few years ago Micky, my brother Neville and I attended her funeral in Shropshire. It wasn't a sad affair because she lived well into her eighties, and she had lived her life to the full. She taught me an awful lot, and she didn't conform to any old lady stereotype. She always saw the best in me, and tried not to judge. In the late 1970s I arrived at her house in fake leopard-skin trousers. She never even blinked. She just said that I should have had a jacket to match. What a woman.

Mrs B lived down this road on the left-hand side,
near where those women are chatting.

Chapter 17

The Chinese guinea pig

The guinea pig fur,
Feeling like silk.
Or the milkman's hide,
Splattered in milk.

Although most of my escapades were with Micky, I occasionally went freelance. There was one experience in particular that brings a smile to my face.

Not far from where we lived was a likeable old character called Fred, and like most old characters he knew everything. He knew all the remedies to all ailments. Unfortunately, the cure for all was his urine. If he had a cold sore he would pee on his finger and dab it on the sore; if he had a cut he would pee on it; if his garden had weeds he would pee on them and if he wanted big vegetables, yes, you guessed it, he would pee on them.

On one occasion I remember delving a little deeper into his theory, and feeling extraordinarily shocked at this story. He told me that his "Old Gal" (his wife) had suffered in later life with leg ulcers, and that he, being a wise, old country medicine man, insisted on removing the bandages and weeing on her ulcerated legs. A few weeks later two of her toes became gangrenous, so he lopped them off with bolt croppers. I was completely mesmerised, and kept up my questioning. "Did the peeing on her leg ulcers work then?", I asked. He replied, "It would have, boy, if she hadn't dropped down dead with blood poisoning".

He could banter with the best of them, and give as good as he got. One day he was chatting with his old cronies, and when I walked by them, he said, " 'ere boy I knew your mother before you were born". As quick as a flash I replied, "You never know, you might be my dad". He thought for a moment, looked me up and down and said, "If I had any kids they wouldn't have been as bloody ugly as you", which made him and his cronies roll about with laughter.

One morning I mentioned to Old Fred that I was looking after some pets, for his neighbours while they were away on holiday. I thought it was an ideal opportunity to wind the old bugger up. I told him that I was very concerned that the neighbours would tell me off when they returned from holiday, because the Chinese guinea pig that I was entrusted to water and feed, had escaped. Fred looked at me quizzically and said, "What the bloody hell's a Chinese guinea pig?" I explained that the guinea pig was about the same size as a basset hound, but I had overfed it, and it was now too big for its cage. I had had to push it from behind, to squash it into its cage. I said that this special breed of guinea pig could burrow underground and pull the vegetables down into its tunnel, and eat them. I was now worried sick, because it had already stripped Old Bob's vegetable patch, and it looked as if it were heading towards Fred's garden. I knew Old Bob was away, so I knew Old Fred couldn't check that out with him. Quite content with such a lovely story I wandered off into the sunset.

The next day I was met by a friend of mine, Paul. He was very anxious, and said, "You are for it. Old Fred nearly killed the milkman with his gun". Old Fred had believed my story hook, line and sinker. He had decided to wait up all night for the Chinese guinea pig to arrive. He had sat among his vegetables with his shotgun, like a Japanese sniper, with a large supply of cigarettes and a few bottles of stout. At 6 A.M. an overtired, slightly sozzled Fred had heard a noise, and opened fire, causing the petrified milkman to dive for cover, smashing a crate of milk.

Fortunately Fred had missed the milkman by a whisker, in fact a Chinese guinea pig's whisker. I kept out of the way of Old Fred and the milkman for a few weeks. A few years later he tried to sell me a so-called antique stuffed squirrel, in an original glass case, and a gun. I was amazed to see that the antique squirrel was really a stuffed rat, with a feather-type object sticking out of its backside, and two of

Fred's broken false teeth protruding from the mouth. The "squirrel" was then inserted into an old fish tank surrounded by garden weeds. The gun turned out to be his old guinea pig hunting rifle with an extremely bent barrel. No wonder he missed the milkman.

Chapter 18

The great white hunter

Shooting a sport,
That I never found funny.
I never killed for pleasure,
Only for money.

I might as well stay on the shooting theme. As I mentioned earlier, in 1974 we had moved from 8 Newcroft into the ordnance depot. The depot was encircled and protected with walls that were over 30 feet in height, and massive wooden gates to match. Running alongside our government-rented house was a cut off part of the Grand Union Canal, which was originally used to carry the old gunpowder barges down to the storage buildings. Obviously this had ceased after the war, and the buildings were used by the Home Office.

Half of the depot was owned by the Home Office and half was owned by the Department of the Environment. My dad worked for the D.O.E., which is why we lived in the house. The total seclusion was the exact opposite of the estate life I was used to. The wildlife was totally unspoilt and incredible. I had my own foxes, badgers, rabbits, kingfishers, herons and swans, which I fed daily. They were beautiful creatures. I would fish daily, and always return the fish, and I would go treasure hunting. The military history was amazing, there were remnants of weapons, military dungeons, pill boxes, spent rounds, and to begin with, it was a young boys dream.

Within the Home Office end of the depot was a large metal canopy overhanging the canal, and I soon discovered that it was constantly frequented by resting pigeons, which used it as an overnight stop. My business brain soon began to work overtime, as I had seen pigeons for sale in the local butcher's window. As far as I was concerned, a pigeon was just a pigeon, no matter whether it was called a wood pigeon or a racing pigeon.

My predicament was quite clear: how could I get the pigeons from the overhang into the butcher's window. I couldn't approach the butcher directly because he would have told my mum. My mother had allowed my brothers to have air rifles, however for reasons of world safety, she had banned me from ever touching one.

After further research I discovered that the local scrap dealer was the supplier of pigeons to the butcher, at a price of fifty pence each. I approached the scrap dealer and struck an agreement that he would give me thirty pence per bird, and no questions asked. My plan was put into action on a fine Saturday afternoon.

My mother was doing the washing, my father was

digging the garden, the little ones were playing, and the Gruesome Twosome, Neville and Andrew, had gone into Northampton. I crept into Neville and Andrews's room and borrowed one of the air rifles, and some lead pellets from the drawer, where they secretly kept their porn magazines. I sneaked past my parental guards and marched off like a soldier going to war. On that first occasion I entered the role whole heartedly, and camouflaged my face with mud, which was not a good idea, for on my return I had forgotten to remove it and had to have a bath. That was a cruel punishment for an eleven-year-old conquering hero, who was soon to be wealthy. In those days I only had one bath a month, whether I needed it or not. In fact the dogs smelled better.

I remember taking aim and shooting the first, poor, defenceless pigeon, and it took four pellets to bring it down. I felt terrible, but greed had taken over. That first time I killed four pigeons, squashed them into my plimsoll bag and walked the four-mile roundtrip journey to claim my bounty of £1.20, which was a lot of money to me. The scrap dealer asked no questions, paid up like a true gent and gave me an old ARP warden's tin hat. This was to be a fitting crown, and anyway a boy could never have too many tin helmets. I wandered home a happy little soldier.

My bounty was invested wisely. I bought ten No 6

cigarettes and two packets of 1/72-scale soldiers. Strangely enough, I still have one of those habits. Yes, I still have my collection of soldiers, forty six thousand at the last count.

My newfound wealth had gained an unhealthy interest from my brothers, but my excuses were in place: "I returned pop bottles, odd jobbing, found it", and many more. My new business venture was flying along; however, like too many business leaders, I became too greedy.

A few weeks later I downed twenty pigeons, using a noticeable amount of the Gruesome Twosome's pellets, and I carried the three bags of squashed birds along the road to the scrap man. I was mentally spending my £6.00 windfall. Much to my surprise the scrap man was in a foul mood. He ranted that in future I would have to remove the racing tags from the pigeon's legs, or he wouldn't accept them. I thought he was being a misery because he didn't like parting with that much money. Our short-lived business relationship had begun to strain.

The following week I did what he had requested, and I removed all the tags, from the birds, and then I handed the birds to him. This time he was even angrier. His words still ring in my ears, "I told you to cut the ******* tags off, not chop their ******* legs off with pliers". Then he said, "How can they hang in a ******* butcher's window if they haven't got any ******* feet". I had to accept a fifty percent reduction on my fee.

I felt so deflated on my walk home that I contemplated looking for other business outlets. How dare the foul-mouthed git of a scrap man talk to a retired ex-catholic, ex-church going, sometimes ex-school-going boy like that. The day could not have got any worse, or so I thought.

I walked through the front door of our house and was leapt on by Neville and Andrew. They had been counting the pellets, and had discovered that I had been stealing them. I wasn't too concerned at the time because they didn't have any evidence. That did not deter them, because they had planted their own.

Neville held a tape recorder microphone, and Andrew held his pump-action pellet gun in one hand, and a half smoked cigarette stub in the other. They expected to extract a full confession out of me, admitting to owning the stub, and admitting to being a regular smoker. The enforced confession was to be taped and used in evidence against me.

What happened next was an early style of court proceedings. Andrew beat me with the gun while Neville attempted a very poor impression of me confessing to the alleged crime. Most people may wonder why I didn't confess to the false charge. Believe me, if you knew my mother, a hiding off them was nothing compared with what she would do. She would have given me a clout, and would have kept me in for at least a month.

They couldn't break me. Andrew made a final attempt; he hit me square in my back with his gun butt, and badly winded me. That reduced me to a breathless, sobbing heap on the floor. My bawling made them pause momentarily, giving me enough time to pounce on a surprised Neville and swipe the cigarette stub from Andrew. I then rammed it into my mouth and swallowed it. They then were without evidence. Strangely enough I now have the tape in my possession, and it was at that time I realised Andrew's vocation in life: He followed my eldest brother Paul into the police force.

The following week I got my revenge. I discovered Andrew's cache of condoms, and I put small pin holes in the packets. I remember thinking two nil to the runt.

Andrew and I would clash many more times. When my friends and I would camp out during the school holidays, we always tried to keep our whereabouts a secret; however, Andrew and his bully boy mates would track us down, rough us up, nick our fags and sweets, and pull our tents down. On one occasion they held me down and covered my face in dog muck. I wasn't allowed back in the tent by my mates until I had washed my face in the river.

It may surprise people to know that I am a wildlife enthusiast and a vegetarian. I thought I should mention that before all the pigeon fanciers cull me. The closure of my pigeon business caused me to diversify into the recycling industry. I was ahead of my time.

Micky and I got up early on Saturday mornings and walked the streets, knocking on doors, asking for old pop and beer bottles. We even invested in a cart. Well not quite, we found one. After a few weeks in business all the pub landlords accepted it as the norm for us to return the bottles to them. We were ticking over nicely. One extremely cold winter morning, it occurred to us that it was too much like hard work. We needed to find a more productive way of doing things.

We watched the landlord from each pub, and discovered where they each kept their empty beer bottles, before collection from the brewery lorries. When the coast was clear we filled our little cart with each pub's empties, and returned them to another pub. Fortunately there were lot of pubs in Weedon. It took the landlords a while to catch on. They knew they were up on some beer bottles; however, they were under on other types. They couldn't understand how it was happening.

We made a small fortune, but as usual we became too greedy. We tried it too often and got caught. The result was that no landlord would accept any bottles, from any children. Yet again Micky and I felt hard done by, so invested some of our profit into buying enough snuff to pour into each pub's fan, each pub's open windows, and the ventilation systems. Money well spent.

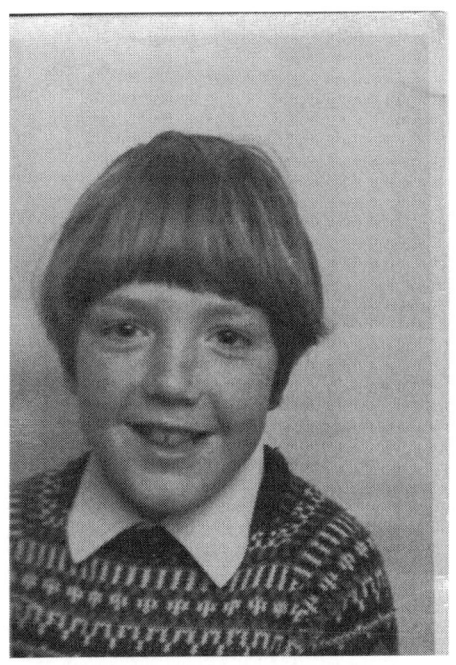

Me after a Gwyn haircut. I said I wanted to look like
Brian Connolly from the band Sweet.

One of the pubs where we returned bottles.

In the centre is the canal that ran alongside our house. I fell into this one.

Chapter 19

Guardian angel

Watch over me,
As I do roam.
Keep me from harm,
And take me home.

After Neville's accident, and during the following many months that he was in hospital, I began to break away from the family and became self-sufficient. My mother quite rightly had to be at his bedside every afternoon and evening; she did not miss one day of hospital visits. We didn't have a car, so she would catch a bus at 10 A.M. and return home at 10 P.M. I knew that it was a terrible financial struggle for my parents, so much so that Neville paid for the headstone on Gwyn's grave. Fortunately he had saved some money while he was in hospital. Obviously meal times went right out the window; it was strange though because I rarely went hungry. When I felt peckish people seemed to know, and they fed me, and not once did I ask.

It wasn't unusual for me to have Yorkshire puddings and mint sauce at Micky's house on a Sunday, chips at Alien's on a Friday, numerous delights at Mrs B's and delightful meals at Pluto's. Pluto was in fact Adam Bewely. He was one of four children, and he had a wonderful home life. His parents were kind, honest, hardworking people, who always gave their children the best, and usually everybody else's kids as well. They were a little different to most of the other kid's parents, because they were buying their own house, and they trusted their children to behave like adults, which we never did. Not one of their children got into trouble with the police.

One evening I was on my way home from their house, when I had a very peculiar experience. I had entered the main depot gates, locked up behind me, and then began the quarter of a mile walk to our house. It may have seemed a very odd thing to do, but I was an odd child, but to pass the time I got into the habit of closing my eyes, walking thirty paces, and then seeing how far I had walked. That evening, for some unknown reason, I decided to close my eyes and walk one hundred paces, which was not a good idea.

I had covered about eighty paces of my blind walk when I felt a falling sensation. I had in fact been walking at an angle, and had walked over the edge of the brick bank, into the canal that ran alongside our house. After falling I remember little, apart from a strange pushing sensation, to get me out of the water.

The canal was only 5-feet deep, however there was decades of sludge at the bottom, and the water was encased by

6-feet-high sheer walls. There was nothing to grab hold of, and nothing to climb onto; the walls were completely flat.

I somehow managed to get out of the sludge, out of the water and scale the sheer walls, and all of that while in shock, wearing a saturated parka and heavy boots. I arrived at home an hour after falling into the water, confused and unsure of what had happened. The following day I looked at my boots, and they were scuff free, and my hands were not grazed. Considering I was less than 5-feet tall, it was incredible good fortune.

On a few traumatic occasions within my life I have experienced a strange feeling of looking at myself from the outside. Many years later I was a passenger in a car, which had a serious accident. The part of the car where I was sitting was crushed. I was found a hundred yards away from the car with minor injuries. I should have been killed. Make of it what you will.

Chapter 20

Raindrops keep falling on my head

If you hear rain,
Walk on by.
Do not look up,
Or you may cry.

As a young teenager my highlight of the week was Sunday
night youth club, which was run by Mr Ogden and a couple
called Dan and Sue. They were very tolerant people, who let us
kids get away with an awful lot. It takes a special kind of
person to give up their free time and energy, look after
strangers' kids and not get paid. Dan and Sue knew we were
tearaways, but also knew that it was mainly because of high
spirits. Dan in particular enjoyed the abuse and play fighting, as
much as we did.

Every year all the youth club children were taken
youth hostelling for an extended weekend. It was a holiday to
some of the kids, and we all looked forward to it. I finished
school at 4 P.M. on Friday, rushed home, got my rucksack,
which contained my sleeping bag and fags, and met the rest of
the lads at the village hall. We then walked the five miles to
Badby youth hostel, and surprisingly enough, we arrived
without any major incidents.

On arrival we visited the local off licence, and we purchased a large quantity of cider, which we soon polished off. We were quite merry, but we weren't too drunk.

Dick managed to pick the lock on the chocolate cupboard, and I raided the girl's sanitary towel machine. The towels made excellent padding for our boots.

After stuffing our faces full of the stolen chocolate, drinking far too much cider, and smoking to excess we all went upstairs to our freezing dormitory. It wasn't too long before Mark felt sick, so we gave him an old bucket to throw up in, and while he was vomiting we added all of Alien's pairs of socks to the bucket. The socks soaked up the cider, and Alien had to walk the following day's 7-mile trek in just bare feet and boots.

Our room had bunk beds against all the walls, and the adults were in another dorm, away from us. Micky had the top bunk, and I had the bottom bunk.

At about 11-ish the cider had started to take its toll, and we all wanted a wee, but none of us wanted to walk down the freezing cold stone steps to the loo. It was soon decided that we would all pee out of the rear window, but a boastful Micky was his usual cocky self. He said, "I'm too big to go out that little window", and he whipped out his frequently exposed thing, and peed out the large, main front window. He was halfway through relieving himself when we heard an almighty scream, and then there was the sound of rushing footsteps up the stone stairs. We all jumped back into our beds, and hid in our sleeping bags. I briefly wondered why we were hiding, until a panicky Micky blurted out, "I have pissed on the wardens head".

The rest of us were shaking with laughter, when a urine-saturated youth hostel warden charged into our room, followed the urine trail, and stood by Micky's bed. His exact words were, "You despicable little urchin, you filthy little swine", and other words that we didn't care to understand.

Dan the youth club leader eventually came into our dorm, from the extremely cold toilet. He looked pale, ill, and his hair was sticking up everywhere. He looked near to death. In fact he was very ill, because unbeknownst to him, we had earlier melted a whole bar of laxative chocolate into his bedtime drink.

The following day Micky, supported by Dan, apologised sincerely to the warden. Because of this incident we were banned from the next trip. In fact we all went on to become despicable little urchins, because a few months later we were banned from the youth club barge trip, for no apparent reason. So we got our revenge by walking the ten-mile journey to the Blisworth barge tunnel, and we patiently waited on top of it. When the youth club barge began entering the tunnel, we jumped to our feet, unzipped our flies and delivered our justice.

The youth hostel where Micky urinated out the window.

Chapter 21

Farming life

Can a dog fly?
Then tell me how.
Just add a hoop,
And then a cow.

It wasn't all play during our early teens. We had to get money for fags, beer and discos, so we all had to find summer jobs. Some of the more fortunate lads got pocket money; however, I had to find work or invent scams.

One way of earning serious money during the summer holidays, was to work for Mr Russell, the farmer. He was a decent fair man who adored the village lads, but despised townies, so I liked him. We were employed to rid the fields of wild oats by hand, and it was extremely hard graft. We used to oat pick in pairs, and we took our sandwiches and flasks up to the fields at 8 A.M. and left the fields at 8:00 P.M. We would have raw hands, and our torsos were burnt from the sun, and quite often we would be dehydrated. We definitely earned our money.

Friday evening was the highlight of the week, as it was pay day. All the pairs of young oat pickers would stand in a queue, accept their pay, nod their heads and thank Mr Russell.

The picker would then move to the side and excitedly count his money. It must have happened in exactly the same way for hundreds of years, before pesticides. On more than one occasion, after the excitement and the boasting of how much we had earned took place, Mr Russell would fill our heads with farming tales.

One Friday evening, he told us how clever his little Jack Russell dog called Rupert was. He said that he could find his rubber toy hoop, no matter where we hid it. We hid that hoop in the hedge, in the hayloft, underneath a cart, underneath the tractor. Every time he found it; he was that good.

After thirty minutes, one of us came up with a brilliant idea. We decided to put the rubber hoop onto one of Rufus's horns. Rufus was a huge brown-and-white bull with a ring through his nose. He was also a good-natured, semi-retired old beast. After a couple of minutes we heard that Rupert had found his beloved ring.

There was stamping, snorting, bellowing and dust flying everywhere. It was a very angry bull, and he was going wild. He shook his head all around. At that point we noticed that a very eager Rupert was holding on to his hoop for dear life, and he was spinning around Rufus's head like a Catherine Wheel. Eventually the hoop and Rupert flew off the angry bull's horn at high velocity and landed in the hedge, and the only thing hurt was his pride. Sadly that was the last year I worked at Mr Russell's farm, because the following year I had to leave school and enter full-time employment.

Chapter 22

The nut factory

Soaking wet,
Wet as a frog.
Eating treats,
Fit for a dog.

The thing about playing tricks on people is that you have to expect them back. Well I did, and I accepted them with good grace. I found that people who couldn't take a joke had very few friends. But I suppose we are what we are.

A regular income was crucial to me, as obviously I needed money for cigarettes. I was always in trouble with my mother for smoking, but it wasn't her money I was spending. I couldn't understand her argument. She would keep me in for smoking, and then I would have to sit in the front room, watching TV all night with the rest of the family. It was a tiny front room with an open coal fire, which belched out thick black smoke. All the doors and windows were shut, and at least five people, three dogs, two cats, and a couple of birds were caged in there at any one time.

My father would sit in silence watching his TV programmes, while we would also sit in silence. His evening consisted of watching TV, chain smoking his Woodbine high-tar cigarettes, interrupted by the odd cup of coffee. Sometimes we struggled to see across the room because of all the smoke. Even one of our dogs, Fred the Basset, had a smoker's cough, and I am certain that all that smoke wasn't good for my little sister Ceri's asthma. I had a worse cough when I wasn't smoking. But at least I had fresh air and exercise if I was allowed out.

To have money for cigarettes, I needed a job, especially through the winter months. One of my mates, Belly, a good lad, helped me in my quest. He landed himself a nice little Saturday morning job at the nut factory. It was an old Victorian factory opposite our old Victorian primary school. The factory supplied all kinds of nuts. There were bird nuts, salted nuts for pubs and nuts for posh people. I had never seen a cashew nut until I went there.

Belly's job consisted of arriving at the factory at 7:00 A.M. and washing all the nut delivery vans. Because the business had grown and they had purchased more vans, Belly needed a van washing assistant. And that is where I came in. I was paid exactly the same wage as Belly, but it made him feel important to call me his assistant.

Belly and I had attended primary school and had played youth football together. He had a good sense of humour and was a bloody good worker. He worked a paper round six days a week and washed vans on the seventh, he was a bit like Jesus, really. Belly was very dark skinned and some of us called him Ghandi, as we thought he might be Indian. Saying that now, might be considered racist, but we certainly didn't mean it to be.

Everyone, in fact, loved Belly. He didn't have any enemies, and anyway I loved Ghandi, as well. He was a good-looking lad, but he didn't have Micky's sexual knowledge, so didn't know what power he had.

Every Saturday morning I would awake at 6:15 A.M., put on my tatty, half-mast flared jeans and my old Levi jacket, and walk the mile down the depot hill to meet Belly. We would meet outside the corner shop and share our first cigarette of the day.

The first Saturday of my new job was most memorable. It was cold, wet and freezing, a typical 1970s winter morning, and I would rather have been tucked up in bed. I nearly resigned before I had started. Belly led me around the corner to the nut factory and introduced me to a couple of people who worked there, as they were doing overtime. There was a middle-aged man with half his teeth missing and a hard looking face. He just stared at me and swore a lot; in fact, that was all he ever did to me. Ironically, his name was Killer. A most suitable name, I thought. The nice thing about him was that he worked inside, and he was happy to stay indoors smoking his cigarettes.

The other person I was introduced to was Peg Knight, who was two years older than me and a mate of my brother Andrew. His real name was Ian, but he had broken his leg as a kid, so was called Peg Leg. He was one of seven kids, part of a family who lived at the top of the village, right near to where my sister Gwyn had moved. I considered them to be one of the most hard-working families in the village. They all worked hard, they still do, all were tough, and Peg was no exception.

Peg worked inside the factory; however, he took far more pleasure in annoying Belly and me outside. Peg was a Weedon boy, and like all the Knight family, if you sliced them in half you would see the word Weedon embossed like a stick of rock inside them. I liked Peg, and so did Belly. We knew he would do things to us, but we knew we could do things back. That was the fun of it. He wasn't a bully, he was a good lad. He was only sixteen and we were only thirteen/fourteen but we respected him. (Years before, Micky and I had been thrown off a bus from Daventry. We were just infant school age, so Peg got off the bus to help us get home.)

On that first Saturday morning Peg double-crossed me and I got soaked with freezing cold water. I double-crossed him and he got soaked, and we both double-crossed Belly and he got soaked. We had a scream. We were all saturated but it was hilarious. Every week was like that, and it was a wonder that we didn't die of hypothermia.

One of the nicest benefits of working at the nut factory was you could eat as many salted nuts as you liked, as long as you didn't get caught. Much to my amazement I discovered that they also supplied tonnes of chocolate buttons. Chocolate was very much a treat for me, so, with the encouragement and blessing of Peg and Belly, I dived in. Being such a greedy pig, I stuffed my face with them every Saturday. I would leave the factory every week feeling sicker and sicker, and of course soaked to the skin.

One day, after about six months, I wandered upstairs in the factory to have my mid-morning chocolate button gorge. The usual sour-faced Killer broke into a smile and his broken fangs were showing. He yelled, "Why are you eating the f****** dog chocs, you stupid t***?". Belly and Peg had told me they were chocolate buttons and I had been had. It wasn't any wonder that they made me feel sick; they tasted like crap. Mind you, my hair had a nice shine to it, and I am sure they helped me run faster.

This is a picture of Belly and me after a morning's work at the nut factory.

I am the one with the Robinson Crusoe trousers.

Chapter 23

Ghost of Weedon Bec

Please stay indoors,
After dark.
The ghouls are roaming,
At large in the park.

Many people during my childhood accused Micky and me of being little bleeders, who were always up to no good. We tried to keep out of trouble, but it always seemed to come to us. When we kicked a ball in the street, you could guarantee a window would get broken, or if we made toast, we would set light to his brother's trousers. We were jinxed. We often tried to walk the straight and narrow path, and we often veered off.

One October morning we had the brilliant idea of going round all the estates, collecting a penny for the guy. We still had our little tow cart, but we didn't have a guy. Micky's mum and dad were at work, and Micky's elder brother Peter was supposed to guard the house, against our mischief making. We considered him to be an unworthy foe, and he was easily manipulated and bribed. Our problem was that we needed some old clothes for the guy; however, Peter was in our way.

We woke a snoring, gorilla-like Peter from his slumber with his favourite breakfast: three pieces of cheese on toast, and a strong mug of tea. I always thought a banana would work just as well. We had played our favourite game of adding as many spices, vinegar, dried mustard and other foreign objects to his tea, to see if his premature failing taste buds would notice. True to form, they didn't. We then made him an offer of ten No 6 cigarettes if he turned the other way, and let us borrow some old clothes from the cupboard. He gratefully accepted.

We delved through all the clothes cupboards, and decided on a nice white shirt, black shoes and a very smart black suit. They were Micky's father's Sunday best. We thought that if something was worth doing, it was worth doing well. We used the lounge cushions to make the body, and we used straw from the rabbit hutch, for his hair. He looked a bit like Bob Geldof.

That evening we trudged around the estates with our well-dressed guy, and we made a fortune. The guy was dressed better than most people in Weedon. With some of our money we bought cigarettes, pop and crisps, and with the remainder we bought a wonderful jet-black outfit, which had a luminous skeleton painted on it. It was out of this world.

Obviously, Micky was the daredevil and the showman, and I could easily manipulate him to do anything. It didn't take me very long to convince Micky that the skeleton outfit looked best on him. As usual, our prank started harmless enough: We knocked on doors, and Micky jumped out to scare the householder, but like all our antics, we went too far. It got to the stage where Micky was jumping in front of cars, and drivers would have to swerve to avoid him. We carried on that prank for a couple of weeks, and the mystery of the skeleton spread. We had incredibly kept it a secret from everyone. In my experience, villages are the best places to spread gossip, rumours and unbelievable tales; therefore, the spooky goings on were more famous than we could ever have imagined.

One dark, foggy, cold Thursday evening a few of us lads urged Micky to go under the main railway bridge, climb up onto the ledge and prance about in his outfit. It was extremely dangerous for a driver, and even more so for Micky. If he had fallen he would have been crushed. We didn't worry about those types of things then; we lived for the moment, and anyway I considered the risk to be worthwhile. Just as Micky had settled on the ledge, I shouted that a car was coming towards us, so me and the lads took cover behind the hedge adjoining the park. Micky was well into his ghostly dance, when the round headlights shone onto his illuminated costume. He looked and sounded fantastic. Fortunately the vehicle wasn't travelling too fast, because the driver managed to slam on his brakes, causing the car to swerve at an angle, and it blocked the road completely. This meant that no cars from either direction could pass, but more important it meant Micky's exit was cut off.

Within seconds, a very shook up, angry police officer jumped out of his nearly crashed car, and dragged Micky down from the ledge. It was the local copper. It was the only time that I have ever heard a ghost saying, "Oh ******* hell it's a pig". It doesn't happen like that on Scooby Doo.

Chapter 24

Wrongful arrest

An easy collar,
Cried the boys in blue.
Guilty until proven innocent,
Free the Weedon two.

I soon realised that as Micky and I got older, our pranks got bigger, and the risks far greater. It was easy to see how people got into trouble. People were far more forgiving when we were pre-teens, but as soon as we became teenagers we were no longer considered mischievous, and we were judged to have the makings of criminals.

It was one of those Friday evenings that most young teenagers go through. There was no youth club; there was nowhere to go; Mrs B was away and it was freezing cold. It was the late 1970s, unemployment was high, and money was even harder to come by. Even the pub trade was suffering, so the landlords were less picky about the age of their customers.

Amid all this hardship, however, Micky and I had stashed away twenty No 6 cigarettes and a crisp, blue five-pound note. I remember thinking that the picture of the Queen on the fiver looked great; the old girl had never looked so good.

We made our excuses to the rest of the gang and pretended to go home, but we really sneaked off to Micky's house and prepared ourselves for the journey into real manhood. We were going to go to the Crossroads Hotel to try and get an underage pint or two. We had to keep it quiet from the others, because they would have ruined it.

We entered the Crossroads Hotel, and it was the most posh place we had ever seen. There was brass everywhere, and it was so clean. The bar staff were immaculately dressed, polite, efficient and very impersonal. It was so different from the local pubs. The hotel staff was not as strict about underage drinking, as long as you were smart, well-behaved, and looked about eighteen, which is what we thought anyway. If we had tried to get served in the pubs we would have been thrown out quicker than a non-spending drunk, besides we were too well known.

If you can picture two young teenagers, wearing '70s platform shoes to increase their heights and mascara added to their bum fluff type moustaches, to give them a thicker look, then that would be us. We walked through hotel reception into the main bar area and stood on the brass foot rail next to the bar. That added another 3 to 4 inches to our heights, which put me up to about 5 feet 2 inches tall. At the same time we stuck out our chests, lit up fags and talked about our imaginary children.

The bar staff looked at each other and laughed when they saw us. I thought that they were just being friendly. But we must have looked a right sight, with our chests sticking out, balancing on a foot rail, talking in gruff voices and mascara running down our faces. I now believe that they just let us stay for their amusement.

After three or four pints of the hotel's finest lager and limes, we bid our farewells and vowed to return. On the way home, we walked alongside the front wall of the depot, congratulating ourselves on our rise to manhood. We were feeling older, more mature and drunkenly wiser. We discussed what we were going to do with certain girls, what work we were going to do when we left school, what cars we were going to get, you know, all the teenage boy, macho rubbish.

Outside the lower gate of the depot was the usual abandoned, knackered old Austin, which somebody from the flats had left behind. It was untaxed, uninsured and not roadworthy. Cars were often dumped there, waiting for the council to take them away. We soon discovered that the car was unlocked, and it was to finish our night off completely. What a stroke of luck.

Micky now decided that I should learn to drive. He ushered me into the driving seat, then pushed the car down the depot hill. As I did not know a brake from a ham sandwich, I built up quite a fair speed. Halfway down the hill I realised the danger of the out-of-control car and turned the vehicle into the kerb. Eventually it stopped.

When Micky caught up with me and the car, we realised the seriousness of the situation and the error of our ways. We began to right our wrong and started pushing the dead weight of the car back up the hill, to where it was originally dumped. It was certainly a lot easier going down, than it was trying to push the thing back up. We spent the next two hours struggling, and after dozens of attempts, falling over, and the car rolling back down the hill, Micky decided that I should use my foot as a stopping device. We huffed and puffed, and moved the car backwards 10 yards, then as instructed I shoved my foot under the front wheel.

By that time we were tired and exhausted, all our energy was sapped, and I had a bloody great car resting on my platform shoe. It was the middle of the night, and panic had set in, and I was completely stuck.

At about midnight a middle-aged man and woman from one of the new estates walked past the car, and I don't know how we managed it, but we were able to persuade them not to call the police as we were just innocent do-gooders. Our story was that we were strolling down the depot hill, taking in the evening air, when out of the blue an unmanned car sped past us. So without any thought for our own safety, we jumped into the road, and stopped the car. It was so convincing that I almost believed it. Fortunately for us they believed our complete drivel, as they were even drunker than we were. They helped us park the car safely, and we thanked our lucky stars before going home.

The following day I got up bright and early, met Micky, and we congratulated each other on such a lucky escape. Mrs B was still away, but had given us permission to go into her empty house during the day. So to celebrate our near-miss I decided we should even fate out a little. I said that we should collect some firewood for Mrs B, saw it, chop it and stack it neatly for her. Micky readily agreed.

At 10:30 A.M. my mother telephoned Mrs B's house and told me to come home immediately, which I did. I walked towards home, where little David and Ceri were waiting for me. They nervously blurted out that the police were waiting for me. They told me to run away and hide, or the police would take me to prison. I believe that was the most loyalty that anyone has ever shown me.

I wondered if I should just come clean about taking the car, and I tried to think of a way of admitting it without incriminating Micky. I sheepishly entered the front room, where the policeman brashly read me my rights. My mother was in floods of over-dramatic tears. She bellowed at me to own up, so as I was just about to confess to my crime, the police officer said, "What have you done with the stolen records?" I hadn't got a clue what he was on about. He went on to say that a large amount of records were stolen from inside a local pub. The disc jockey had seen us in the area earlier, and presumed that we had returned and nicked them from the back room.

While the policeman gave me verbal abuse, my mother wailed, "How could you do such a thing, you have let the family down". I never knew we were up. Mind you, she had every right to be hysterical, as most people could not have coped with what had happened in her life. She was still grieving for Gwyn, nursing Neville, and nursing dad, and still had to find time to look after the little ones.

I pleaded my innocence, but could not give a concrete alibi, because at the time in question my foot was underneath a stolen car. The policeman eventually left, with a promise that he would be back later to take me away. I returned to the safety of Mrs B's house.

Yet again I felt hard done by, nobody would listen to me and no one would believe me. It was just after 3:00 P.M. when I was summoned again, by an even angrier, more hysterical mother. "What is it this time?" I cried, and she said that another policeman was at the house, accusing me of another crime. I began the walk of shame, for a second time, and that time I thought it would relate to the moving of the vehicle. I entered the front room and was met by a younger, more understanding and more civil police officer. The charge he stated was again a complete shock; he accused us of slashing the corner shop awnings. Believe it or not, but that crime also took place at the same time as the record theft and at the same time as the car was stuck on my foot. I again couldn't give him a convincing alibi.

After twenty minutes of his questioning and my mum's sobbing, the policeman put me in his car and drove me round to Mrs B's house, as he wanted to interrogate Micky. The young copper certainly sounded and looked the part, until he rang Mrs B's doorbell, and Micky opened the door wielding a large, wood chopping axe. The poor policeman turned green with fear, and staggered backwards. I had to sit him down with a cup of tea and a fag, to calm his nerves. He was actually a very nice bloke, in fact too nice. I should imagine he has been promoted to the rank of police dog by now.

For the record, both charges against us were dropped. The DJ's records had been hidden by his friend, as a prank, and two lads from another village were charged with damaging the shop awnings. We did not receive any apologies from the police, but we put the hassle down to karma. Pay back for nicking the car.

The hill where the car got stuck on my foot.

The Crossroads Hotel where we had our first grown up drinks.

Chapter 25

School bullies

When do the bullies,
Stop having fun?
When the tables are turned,
And it's their turn to run.

I discovered that no matter what school or place of employment you attend, there will always be bullies. Bullying is not always blatantly obvious, but it is there. When I had first arrived at Bugbrooke Campion Comprehensive School, I knew there was something very interesting down the loos, because my head kept getting shoved down there. I really couldn't understand what the older kids got out it. There was no gain, so I couldn't see any reason for the process. As I was one of the shortest kids in my year I just accepted it.

Primary school had been so different, everyone knew each other, and usually we all got on. At senior school it was awful, as the kids were bigger and nastier, and the teachers were less tolerant. I soon realised that it was a dog-eat-dog world, and found that by having a sense of humour, you could avoid some of the horrors. I remember my hair being set alight by a Bunsen burner once. All the kids laughed, so I did it again and again. For six months I looked like Michael Jackson.

It could have been worse, though. There was another small kid in our year, and unfortunately his surname was Mole. During the rural studies lesson the bigger kids used to lock him in the chicken run with a spade. His job was to kill as many rats as he could, and they wouldn't let him out until he had killed three. I remember one naïve girl screeching, "Sir, Sir, come quickly, Mole is fighting with the rats again". It was a scream.

After Gwyn's tragic death, and Neville's accident my misdemeanours became worse and my interest in lessons started to decline. Mum was at the hospital every day, caring for Neville; Dad would go straight from work and look after little David and Ceri; Andrew was preparing to go into the forces and Paul was in a police force, miles away. I was going wayward.

I remember clearly what the final straw was. My mother informed me that Dad, (with whom I had shared a bedroom for the previous three years), was terminally ill with lung cancer. He used to keep me awake every night with his poor breathing and his restless nights. I always thought it was something to do with his malaria or asthma, but to find out that he had been slowing dying of cancer in the next bed to me, was heartbreaking. I felt so sorry for him, and I couldn't do anything to ease his suffering. That previous three or four year period was more than I could cope with; it didn't seem fair. I worried about the house finances, and I worried more so about little Ceri and little David. My father adored them, and they adored him.

The kids in my class at school began to refer to me as a Jonah. They started to joke that they didn't want me around because I was bad luck, and I had started to believe it. At that point I changed, I turned from being bullied, into a bully. Micky and I borrowed money from other pupils, and we never repaid. It was really a collection round. We targeted the more affluent boys, and borrowed money on a regular basis. I had become everything I despise. I regret many things in my life, but none more so than that. I am deeply ashamed of it.

There was one lad in particular. He was a shopkeeper's son, and he supplied us with money, fags and fireworks. It was a terrible time for him. Eventually he plucked up the courage to tell his father, and his father confronted Micky's dad. Micky got a telling off and was told to repay an agreed amount. I, on the other hand, was given a message from the lad's father, saying he wouldn't inform my mother because she had enough to cope with. I am eternally grateful that they didn't tell my mother, because it meant my father was never to know.

Over the next few months I willingly gave the boy all my school dinner money, and my Saturday morning job

146

money. The boot was on the other foot, and I was pleased. I didn't want my father's last memories of me to be as a bully, and I believe that second chance changed my life. Later in life I was to be paid back with interest. Things usually even themselves out.

I saw much bullying at school, none worse than was committed by some girls. Those girls seemed to be far more ruthless, and they bullied for no other reason than that they were jealous. They bullied one girl in particular, a slightly younger girl. They verbally abused her in public, and then they all took turns at beating her up. We boys tried to intervene, but that didn't stop them. She certainly was a plucky lass, because she fought back against all of them. There were far too many of them, however, and they had the mental edge. She never reported them to anyone, but one night it became too much for her, and she took an overdose of pills. Thank God she survived, but has led a troubled life since, and she still carries the mental scars.

A little later in my school career, another strange event occurred. Micky and I were minding our own business one day, going down some school stairs, when an art teacher, with whom I had got on very well, came rushing down the steps and threw me into the wooden stair rail. The rail hit the base of my spine, and I crumpled to the floor in agony. (It still gives me discomfort now.) He then tried to grab Micky, but Micky was ready for him, and grabbed his arm, and then pushed him away. The teacher then blurted out that we had been bullying a boy in his form, and the boy had pointed us out. At that exact moment a small boy with ginger hair shouted, "Not them two, the two at the top of the stairs". The teacher wouldn't look me in the eye. He just left the scene, extremely embarrassed. I put the injury down to divine retribution.

After the closure of our collection business I concentrated on my more serene scams. I was always gambling, or buying and selling, anything to make a few quid. And while I am owning up to some of my misdemeanours I would like to confess and apologise to my teachers for the following: In 1978 the school fire alarm went off. That was me accidentally causing a fire in the girls' toilets. I didn't put out my cigarette properly in the faulty sanitary towel incinerator. Also in 1978 the school Christmas disco was vastly overcrowded, because I hand-forged an extra hundred tickets and sold them at a quarter of the price. On my last day of school in 1979, I was made to stand in front of the school, covered in eggs and flour. I had said to the headmaster that I was ambushed and attacked by unknown pupils; however, that wasn't the case. I was in fact covered by friends, but couldn't inform on them.

Informing to the powers that be, was always frowned on, and to my knowledge we only broke the code once. Next to river, in Bridge Street, lived a lovely old man called Mr Boys. One night he was attacked by teenagers with two lumps of wood, and he never fully recovered. The day after the attack, the local policeman lined up a group of us, and threatened to throw us in the canal if we didn't tell him who committed the terrible crime. He didn't need to do that, as he should have known better. We all liked Mr Boys, and mugging old people was not our style.

Within twenty-four hours, we had done his job for him. We interrogated all the other kids and tracked down the culprits. We gave the names to the police. It was lucky for them that we didn't get them first.

Micky and I were petty thieves. We took from shops, and we could pick any type of padlock with a bent wire. It was in Bridge Street that I remember a time in the very early '70s when we climbed over the old chapel fence, through the butcher's window, and into the rear of the corner shop, to drink the bottles of pop. Strangely, we never took the alcohol, groceries or money. Mind you, we were only seven years old. As we entered the window Micky tripped on a curtain, and landed on his head. He was knocked out for what seemed to be an eternity. I obviously waited by his side and drank all his pop. One of my brothers now owns the old chapel and the old butcher's shop, and the first thing he did when he bought them, was brick up our entrance window; however, thirty-three years too late.

I look at kids now, wandering the streets, looking lost and getting into trouble, and I feel sorry for them. They feel that there is nothing for them, and often adults don't have enough time to guide them. The only difference between me and the kids in the remand homes, is that I was lucky, because I never really got caught for the more serious offences. I often say, "There but for the grace of God go I". If I had been charged with a crime, I am sure that my life would have turned out differently. Some of today's children have far more problems than we had to deal with: They have too much time, too much money and drugs to contend with. I wouldn't want to return to my childhood, not for all the money in the world.

At the left of the picture is the shop from where we took the pop. The gap between the buildings on the left side is where the Church was, where Micky had his only religious experience.

The shop where dear old Mr Boys lived.

Chapter 26

The light-blue suit

A fashion leader,
Or a tasteless sod.
Nothing could stop me,
Becoming a mod.

In 1979 I was sixteen years old. I didn't have a gradual change from boy to man, it was overnight. I sometimes feel that I was never a child, and that I was born into an adult world. Then other times I feel that I have never become a man, and that I am still a child. I feel that vulnerability.

A day after my sixteenth birthday I left school, and the following day I began work in a steelworks. It was not an enjoyable experience. But for the meagre sum of £20.55 per week, what was a boy to do? It was quite ironic really, because I hated metalwork at school, but the job was walking distance from home.

When I went for the job interview I wore a light-blue, made-to-measure suit. Unfortunately, it was made for someone else, and not for me. It was, in fact, made-to-measure for my old dad, and was his work suit, which had been tailored at Burtons. Dad always wore a suit; he was well-turned out. The old boys then always made an effort, polished shoes and ties, even in the hottest summers. Dad was only 5 feet tall and had a 26-inch waist, so when I wore his suit I resembled a very young Norman Wisdom.

Everything in life is about timing. I found that one had to try and salvage something good out of every bad situation. For example, it was devastating to me that because my dad was dying he gave me his suit. But on the plus side, the Mod revival and its music had started a few months before, and my suit was the same colour as the suit wore by Sting in the film Quadrophenia. So I had my hair dyed blonde, wore two-tone shoes, a black trench coat and my light-blue suit. I was to be the Weedon version of The Face, all 5 feet 3 inches of me.

I had very mixed feelings about that suit. I loved it and I hated it. The reason I hated it was because it made me think of some of my father's last words to me. It was a Friday, and I had to go for my interview at the steelworks. I didn't have any decent clothes, only my old army trousers, a pair of my brother's hand-me-down Rupert the Bear trousers (yellow-checked) and a fancy-dress American Indian costume. I could hardly turn up as a bloody soldier, a bear or a sodding Apache Indian, could I? My mother suggested that I ask my dying, bed-ridden father, who was constantly on oxygen, if I could borrow one of his suits to wear for the interview. My poor father who was in intense agony shouted the following words, "You are a vulture who cannot wait for me to die". Nothing was further from the truth. I walked away, went to my bedroom and sobbed. I just wanted him to be proud of me, not angry. I so wanted him to know that I was going straight into employment, and that I was going to bring money into the house.

Life was such a disappointment, then. Actually disappointment was the wrong word. I hadn't expected anything from life, and I didn't get anything from it. It was an emotionally painful time. After what happened to Gwyn I swore that I would never be hurt like that again. I have tried to distance myself from getting too close to anyone or anything since. Later that day my mother said Dad wanted to speak to me. I of course thought I was going to get another telling off and prepared accordingly. I wasn't going to let him see me cry.

I remember looking at that tiny, frail, old man, covered in cancerous lumps and felt such heart-breaking pity for him. I wish I could have been braver and ended his misery. He smiled from his bed and said, "You can have my suit, son, now go and try it on for me". That was his beloved suit, and he gave it to me. He knew he wasn't going to wear it again. I wore that suit every day for months. Not only because I was a fashion god, but also because it still smelled of my dad. While I was wearing that suit, he was with me.

One of the local bullies thought it was great sport to ridicule me. He would make the other kids laugh by saying I was wearing my dead Dad's suit. I would have rather he punched me in the face than ridicule the suit. To me it wasn't just a suit; it was my dad's suit. Dad was the bravest man that I have ever known. It is easy for people to ridicule grieving souls when they have never felt the pain of losing someone. Twenty years later I bumped into the mouthy bully. He had just lost his father and he was hurting. I looked into his tear-filled eyes and paid my respects. I always thought that I would take some pleasure, but I didn't. I just felt sadness.

The Weedon Face.

Who says you can't make a silk purse out of a sow's ear?

One for the ladies, and perhaps a couple of the guys.

Chapter 27

Free from pain

Let him go,
Let him sleep,
He is free from pain,
And we shall weep.

I would like to say that the following was a distant memory or a blur, but it isn't. It feels just like yesterday. It was a Saturday and my dad was very weak. My mother told me to go out because Dad needed peace and quiet. So I decided to meet up with some of the boys, and we caught the bus into Northampton. We all had our suits on, and we were going to strut our stuff in the Grosvenor Centre. We thought we looked great but looking back we must have looked a sight. We believed we were rebels, so we tried to look mean.

While we were walking around record stores trying to catch the eye of some young ladies, we unfortunately caught the attention of some different long-haired creatures. Yes, bikers, greasers, our so-called arch enemies. They were dressed in leather, with greasy hair, spots and tattoos. They looked like they could do with a bloody good wash, which was hypocritical of me, as I had only recently started to wash on a daily basis. (But as I say, "You are only as clean as your last wash".)

The bikers wanted to talk to us more than we wanted to talk to them. There were six of us and hundreds of them; well, actually there were twelve of them, but it felt like hundreds. They encircled us and proceeded to bring out their motorbike chains. I am not a mechanic but I knew they weren't going to do any repairs in a record shop. We had three options: a) stand and fight, b) run and c) stand there and say nothing. Fortunately my brave comrades also had the same idea. We knew we couldn't run because we would have been called cowards, and also my brother Neville was on crutches, so we couldn't leave him. I wish I could say that I turned into a hero and gave them a thrashing, but that did not happen. Instead, just like in an old spaghetti western, a man in his forties walked straight up to the biggest biker and grabbed him. The biker and his mates scattered. The old boy had fronted them out and they were scared.

The highs and lows of that day were incredible. One minute up, the next minute down. We all clambered on the next bus and rode out of town, like the "Magnificent Six". We planned to meet up later .When I returned home, my mother said Dad was still sleeping so it was best if I went out again. I will regret that decision for the rest of my life.

I went to a party in Bugbrooke, but felt totally uneasy. I said to my friend Greg that something felt wrong and that I needed to go home. The pair of us walked the 5 miles home. When I got home I opened the front door, and noticed all the lights were out. There was a deathly quiet and not even the dogs came to greet me. It was the first time that I ever heard total silence. I walked slowly into the front room to say goodnight to Dad, but his bed wasn't there. His oxygen tanks had gone and he was nowhere to be seen. It was like he had never been there. The dogs looked strangely sad, and Ben the Basset was crying, whimpering with real tears. They were in mourning. I ran towards the stairs where my brother Andrew was standing. He was only about seventeen at the time and was on leave from the military. He looked at me and said, "Dad is dead and they have taken him away". He then returned to bed. I stood in that hallway totally alone, no one to talk to, no one to share it with, and no one to grieve with. I still feel that standing alone feeling now. I was barely sixteen.

The next day I got up early and went downstairs. I just wanted some reassurance, someone to talk to and some adult words of wisdom. But to this day I cannot explain why the following happened. My mother and I were talking, and then she lifted up her right arm and slapped me around the face. I didn't feel the physical pain, but the emotional hurt has stayed forever. Surely you shouldn't want to keep hitting someone you are supposed to love? That was the last time I allowed myself to be hit by her. I turned around and walked away from my home. I walked all day, and then found myself at the door of Dan and Sue, the youth club leaders. They answered the door, and I burst into tears. They ushered me in, and I am eternally grateful for that act of kindness. That night I was going to take my own life.

After hours of talking I slept on their sofa, and slept there for two more nights, as my mind was in such turmoil. On the third day the front door burst open and in walked my three elder brothers. I would have said, "Here come the three little pigs", if I hadn't been so upset. They were hardly the three wise men bearing gifts, either; they were more like the three stooges who came to give me a good hiding.

My eldest brother Paul convinced me to come home and make peace with my mother. He told me to return and apologise to her. To this day I do not know what I was apologizing for. Actually, I only said sorry just so that I could attend the funeral of my poor old dad.

The funeral was a couple of days later, and I had managed to immerse myself into alcohol during all that period. It was easier then to get your hands on alcohol at an early age. It was seen as acceptable if you had left school and doing a man's job, then you were entitled, almost expected to drink and smoke.

I remember standing in Saint Peter's Church, Weedon. I stood upright, to attention, just as Dad had told me to do in the school plays. He always said, "Stand tall and push your chest out; be proud". I wore his light-blue suit, and I could smell him. (I shouldn't think there are too many people who go to their father's funeral wearing his suit. Mind you, I have always been a bit odd.) When I stood in that church something happened. I tried so hard to hold the tears back, but they just would not stop. My face was flooding.

We went from the church to the graveyard around the corner. I stood back from the others and watched. I watched my mother throw herself onto the coffin in a dramatic fashion, and I watched as they pulled her off. They lowered his tiny little coffin into the ground and that was that. A lovely gentle old Irish man called Jimmy Mcdonald put his hand on my shoulder and whispered, "You will be alright, Chrissy Boy". He was a good man and a good friend to my father, and I thought the world of him. Jimmy and I had quite a lot in common. He was coming to the end of his life with an alcohol problem and I was just beginning mine with one. Alcohol was to be my drug of choice, along with tobacco of course.

The fond memory I take from that day was when I returned home. My mother, a few of my father's colleagues, Uncle Glyn and the rest of us were having tea and sandwiches, the usual funeral food, when there was a knock at the door. Standing there was a retired Sergeant Major called Sandy. (He became a Chelsea pensioner, shortly thereafter.) He was a tough, hard man, but he was sobbing like a child. He said he had witnessed the horrors of the Sudan and the trenches of the Great War and had not shed a tear. But he said that when he saw me sobbing it released a trigger. It is strange how we all have a weak spot.

I knew then that I had to step up. I was sixteen and I had a job. Mum was looking after little David and Ceri, Neville was recovering from his motorcycle accident, Paul was in the police force and Andy was in the military. I felt like I had a ton weight on my shoulders. I am not saying I had, I am just saying that is how it felt.

My dad is on the left. He had just returned from Burma.

Chapter 28

A man's world

Hang him up,
Punch him twice.
Scald his head,
He's scared of mice.

I wish I could say that my introduction into the work place was wonderful, but I cannot. It was hell on Earth. It was a steelworks for goodness sake, what was I thinking? I had hoped that they would all be the sensitive flower-arranging types, but, alas, they were not.

My official job title was Trainee Apprentice sheet metal worker and fabricator. I don't recall doing any of that. I was in fact the errand boy, paint sprayer, tea boy, laundry boy, punch bag and general dog's body. My daily routine was to cut up loads of metal, and that is about as exciting as I can make it sound. Then I would go around to each of the dozen workers and take their shop orders. I would then waddle off to the Jesus people's (Christian organisation) fruit and vegetable shop and purchase their rolls, etc. On return I would make them hot tea in an urn, so they could relax and be waited on by me.

All but one of those fully grown men hit me during the following few months. One in particular beat me constantly. He beat me for not warming up the tea pot; he beat me for not getting the rolls he wanted, even if the shop had sold out of them. He even hit me for not standing close enough to him when he wanted to punch me. He was an evil bully and he wondered why nobody liked him.

Shortly after I started there I discovered that he had broken an ankle of the previous staff member who had done my job. It seems that he had tried to run away and the bully had thrown a chunk of metal at him.

I tried standing up to him but he was bigger and stronger, and then he would hit me even harder. I knew things were not going to get any better, so I had to find other ways to beat him. One day, the men thought they were being clever by hanging me up by my overalls in the paint-spraying room. I hung there for four hours, not working. I dangled and smoked my No 6 cigarettes all afternoon. I even had a lovely little sleep.

Another task they made me do was empty the factory mouse traps. They knew I liked animals and they knew I hated doing it. One time they gathered all the dead mice and impaled them on thick wire. They then pushed the wire into the wooden door frame of the toilet cubicle that I was sitting in. They thought it was hilarious that I sat in that toilet all day and wouldn't come out because of the mice. What the w****** didn't realise was that I had my sandwiches, cigarettes, the Sun newspaper and two cans of Coke stuffed down my overalls. It was another lovely skiving day, my best day there. You may ask, "What does a sixteen-year-old boy do for six hours in a toilet cubicle with a copy of the Sun newspaper?" Well, I became very close to Linda Lusardi on Page 3 that day. If the bloke from the Guinness Book of Records had been there, then I would have broken the world record.

My weekly wage was £20.55. I had to give my mum £10.00; £5.00 went towards my holiday fund and £5.55 for my cigarettes, clothes, beer and sweets for the following week. I wasn't a man and I wasn't a boy; I was neither fish nor fowl. Because money played such an important part in my life, I had to think of other ways of making it. While I walked down to the Jesus people's shop one day, I had a brilliant idea. I thought that if I tell all my work enemies that there had been a price increase, I could then pocket the change. I increased bread rolls from 4p to 5p, filled rolls from 30p to 35p, Coke from 10p to 12p, etc. I then spoke to the shop manager and asked him if they could give me a discount each day, because I spent so much money with them. I really think he agreed because he felt sorry for me. I always went in there covered in oil, paint, grease and any substance the others threw on me. I even had swear words scrawled on my face with marker pens. I was always bruised and holding back tears. Not tears of pain, but tears of anger, hurt and frustration. Those Jesus people were really good, kind, considerate people.

My new business venture thrived. I went to the shop twice a day, five days a week and at least twenty days a month. That meant I earned at least an extra tenner a week. I received an instant 50 percent pay rise. Like most of my schemes, though, I hadn't thought about the consequences, or I didn't really care about them. Everything was perfect for a few months, until I got punched in my shoulder and had to visit a physio. That meant someone else had to complete the shop run. And that is when they discovered my scam. When I returned from the physio I got the biggest hiding ever. I tried to convince them that they must have gone on a sale day, but the men weren't having any of it. I will admit that I did deserve that hiding, but I just saw it as a failed business venture.

The next day I entered the steel works and I noticed the bully was hunched over his machine. He didn't raise his head to swear at me, he didn't reach into my pocket to steal a cigarette and he didn't even hit me. It took me by surprise. I thought he must have a hangover or something. I soon found out what was up. One of the other morons told me to keep out of his way, because the bully had accidentally made his wife pregnant and he wasn't too happy about it. In fact, he was very angry about it.

The previous evening my friends and I had been in the Crossroads Hotel and had invested some of our money in those very thick condoms: the ones that could be purchased from the gents' toilet. They were lovely colours and with spines on the end like a hedgehog. (There was never going to be a time when I used them because they were massive. I could have fitted one on my big head and I would have looked like a cockerel, and it still would have been too big.) So I thought that the little, or should I say massive, beauty would be put to good use. While making the tea I decided to open the bully's ham-salad roll, and underneath the lettuce I placed the oil-covered condom.

It was the best laugh I had given myself in ages. He bit into the roll and pulled back his head to chew through the ham. When he gave an extra tug from the roll, the thick rubber condom hung from his mouth. It looked like a giant dog's tongue. Everyone laughed at him, and I laughed the loudest. He jumped from his seat and punched me full force, knocking me to the ground. Yet I still laughed and laughed hysterically. The more he hit me the more I laughed. The others by that time had stopped laughing, as they could see he was going too far. I didn't care, and I laughed louder. He then picked up the tea pot and tipped the scalding contents over my head. The pain was awful and I had to soak my head in cold water for hours. After a couple of weeks all the blisters had healed, but I still think it was worth it.

Chapter 29

First love

The beat of a heart,
The coo of a dove.
You hear all these things,
When you are in love.

As mentioned before, £5.00 of my meagre salary went towards my holiday fund, which would be my first all-lads holiday, boys on tour kind of stuff. Everyone at that time was going to Spain and Greece and all those far-off places, with different girls every night and 24-hour drinking. So where do you think my two mates and I were going? Torquay, bloody Torquay. We had booked a smashing two-bedroom holiday apartment in a complex full of what we considered to be elderly people. The choice was not mine.

Two weeks before we were due to go away fate took my hand and gave it to my first true love. It was a Thursday evening when a local lad popped his head into the Malsters Arms pub on West Street. He excitedly told us that a load of teenage girls were on a barge holiday, and they had moored their boats at the Narrow Boat Inn. The inn was more than a mile away but we covered that distance in minutes. I knew how the country girls felt when the GI's arrived during the war.

With me were three other lads, and I was just coming up to seventeen years old. We weren't bad-looking lads, but we weren't as streetwise as we thought, and we were rough around the edges. We entered the inn with cigarettes dangling from the corners of our mouths, and we couldn't believe our eyes. There must have been twenty girls, who were all attractive and aged eighteen. They had just finished their A levels and were having a narrow boat holiday before they went off to university. The holiday was funded by their parents. They spoke well and were well educated.

I was impressed. I didn't know anyone who had been to university, and I only knew one person who went to grammar school. The other three lads had more confidence and they went bombing in. They tried to chat up one girl named Helen. She had long dark hair, blue eyes, white teeth, and I thought she was the most beautiful girl in the world. The other lads soon found out she was not interested, as she was in a relationship with a sailor. They then moved on to chatting up the other girls. I stood back, feeling very awkward and shy. I wasn't used to chatting up posh totty. I was sort of alright with local girls, but I had my working-class insecurities hanging over me. I felt I wasn't good enough for them; I felt beneath them.

After a while a strange thing happened. Helen got up from her table and sat by me. She started talking to me as an equal. We chatted about everything, about the places she had been to and the places I hadn't been to but would love to go. I still feel that moment more than thirty years later. I then realised how love was such a powerful emotion. She could have chosen anyone in that pub to speak to, but she chose me.

When the pub closed, the girls invited us back to one of the boats. I am not sure if it was alcohol or the hormones, but I ended up holding Helen's hand. I was a total love-struck puppy. While we were lying on her very small bunk, our eyes met and we moved our heads towards each other to kiss. I suddenly stopped and asked her if it was okay to do so. There I was, in a compromising position, on a girl's bunk, and I stopped during the most romantic embrace of my young life to ask permission. I could not believe she wanted me.

That night we just lay until 5:00 in the morning, holding each other, talking and gently kissing. I left her to sleep and ran home to get ready for work. I was truly in love for the very first time. Work dragged on that day, but it didn't matter, as I was going to see my beloved Helen again in the evening.

The lads and I met up with the girls at the Longboat Inn at Braunston. Not once did I think about or care that Helen had a boyfriend in the Navy. I was in love and that was all that mattered. We were inseparable in the pub. We just sat staring into each other's eyes, smiling and whispering. We were oblivious to the others talking and teasing us. That night we went back to the boat and just lay together until the sun came up. I returned home, but I couldn't eat or think of anything else but Helen. It was just like how love is in the black-and-white movies. We exchanged telephone numbers, spoke every evening and arranged to meet the following weekend. She lived more than two hours away from me, and it might as well have been in another country. I didn't drive, I didn't have my own place and I had never brought anyone home to stay before.

Everything, however, started to slot into place. First, I asked my Mother if it was okay for Helen to stay in the spare room. Second, I made sure I had enough money to take her out on the Friday and Saturday nights, and still have enough money to go on my two-week holiday with my mates. We were scheduled to leave in the early hours of Sunday morning.

On the Friday Helen arrived in a brand new car. It was present for her eighteenth birthday bought by her parents. Here was a girl who was going off to university, her parents owned their own house and had bought their daughter a brand new, bloody car. There I was, living on a council estate and only owning two pairs of footwear, work boots and my best shoes. (I am ashamed of myself now for that snobbery.) (I of course lied) about us owning our council house, and I also didn't answer questions regarding my dad. I was ashamed to tell her that my dad was dead, as if it were something bad. I didn't want her sympathy. She soon found out the truth.

That night I took her to the classy Crossroads Hotel, where we had a bar snack and a couple of drinks. I had never eaten in a restaurant before and it was nerve-racking, and very expensive. I couldn't take her home for dinner because I had seen the way she had looked at our pet dogs and our house. I'm sure she didn't mean to offend me, but a look can say a thousand words. After we had dined on scampi and chips we went for a drive in her car. (It is funny how I remember my first dining experience better than my first sexual experience. Perhaps because it lasted longer, tasted better and it didn't have Micky groaning away in the same room.) The sexual experience had happened a few months previous, when two girls took Micky and I to a room and used us for their pleasure. I was too nervous, and she was too big, so there wasn't any sensation whatsoever. Micky was humping away quite merrily on the other bed , grunting like a moose. I discussed my failure with Micky afterwards, and we both decided that as I didn't feel then it didn't count.

Helen said she would finish with her sailor boyfriend and would be with me. We kissed and cuddled in the car and went back to my home to our separate rooms.

The next day for breakfast, I gave her tea from the

V.G. shop and frozen chips cooked in lard. I cannot believe I did that. She was probably used to muesli and orange juice. No wonder she looked so shocked. But I had not had anyone to stay over before. I soon discovered that I only had £10 left to wine and dine her for the whole day, and for my holiday.

During the day we walked across the fields, and our hormones built up nicely. I knew it was only a matter of time before the inevitable happened. I stuck to the winning formula of dining at the Crossroads Hotel, and then off for a drive in her car. The sexual attraction was intense, and we couldn't keep our hands off each other. Eventually we decided to park up in a wonderfully secluded, romantic spot. It was the lay-by next to the cemetery.

We were so engrossed in each other's firm, young bodies that it didn't matter where we were. We were young and making proper love for the very first time. It was a warm summer's night, and the windows of the car were totally steamed up. We were completely entwined, both naked. During the final throes of passion I heard a Scouse accent shout through the window, "Hurry up and finish", and an Aussie accent yell, "C'mon we have got to get a move on": my mates, Scouse Paul and Aussie Perry. They had seen the tail lights on the parked car and decided to investigate. They had come to get me for our long trip to Torquay. Perry had insisted that we leave at midnight, and I had lost all track of time. Honestly, I wasn't too bothered by the interruption, but Helen was very upset. I gave her a kiss goodnight, got in the car with the boys and said I would ring her from sunny Torquay.

I hope that is a cigarette lighter in my pocket.

I thought I looked good in those trousers. But on reflection,
I resembled a younger version of Geoffrey from Rainbow.

Chapter 30

The English Riviera

Was there sunshine?
Were we in heaven?
No, just plenty of rain,
We were in Devon.

I had no idea why Paul, Perry and I were going Torquay. I certainly hadn't voted, or if I had, nobody took any notice.

Paul was originally from Liverpool and was a typical Scouser. He had a good sense of humour, loved music, loved Liverpool football club and could look after himself in a fight. He had moved to Weedon four years previously, and I took an instant liking to him. I had a fellow Liverpool football fan at long last. He was a proper supporter; he had been to hundreds of matches. I, however, had only ever seen them play on the old black-and-white television, with my dad.

I sobbed when Charlie George scored that winning goal for Arsenal in 1971 against Liverpool, and I danced with joy when three years later Liverpool beat Newcastle United 3–0. I loved sharing that football time with Dad; it was our time. When Dad died my love for watching the game died. Paul taught us all the football songs and I shared my love of singing Simon and Garfunkel songs with him. We were often found singing some tuneful duets under the railway arches. The great thing was that no one took the p*** out of our singing because Paul, being a city boy, had perfected the art of the head butt. Although Paul could fight well, he was never a bully. That was the sign of a true fighter.

Perry was also a nice guy, but he was very serious. He was honest and hard working, but was totally grown up, unlike me. He and Paul were slightly older; they were already eighteen. Perry had been born in Weedon and then emigrated to Perth, Australia, when he was a kid, along with his sister (Vanessa), his brother (Nicky), and his mum and dad. When Perry turned sixteen, they returned. He was extremely sensible and had a slight tendency to moan. He had strong views, knew what he wanted from life and he was going to get it, he even had a pension. I, on the other hand, just wanted to enjoy myself and be loved.

Perry worked shifts at British Timken and earned some serious money. Paul worked at Foilwraps and also earned some good money. I was the only one of our group who didn't earn much. And I was the only one not to have very much money for the holiday.

Perry recently had passed his driving test, and had bought a big, green, very smart Ford Cortina. It was a proper grown-up car, certainly not the usual first-time-buyer's car. I am certain Perry had planned the holiday down to the last detail. He was responsible for collecting our money weekly, paying the deposit, making all the bookings, and basically doing everything. Paul and I were useless and did none of the planning. If it had been left to us two we wouldn't have got past the first pub. Perry was our policeman; Paul and I just went with the flow.

Along with our weekly holiday saving we had been contributing towards our food money and our petrol money. The three of us were like an old married couple. Perry had even designed a chart stating on which days we would eat certain foods, which days each of us would do the washing up, and what meals we would have on particular days. We even had a bloody house-cleaning rota. Perry issued our first day's instructions: they consisted of us studying the lay of the land, buying groceries and settling in. The second day was a visit to Paignton Zoo; the third day was equally bizarre. It was like going on a two-week school trip. We even went to a bloody waxworks dummy museum of Doctor Who. This wasn't the rock-and-roll holiday I was expecting. As a previously retired Mod, I wanted birds, booze and music. Instead we ended up in something that resembled a retirement home.

When we first entered the holiday apartment we were greeted by the smell of polish and old people. I also caught a whiff of urine, but that was probably me. It was practical and clean. I know we weren't the Wild Bunch but I expected something a little raunchier. There were two bedrooms in the apartment. Bedroom one had a double bed in it; bedroom two had two single beds. That decision was easy: Paul and I nabbed the two single beds and Perry took the double. The first couple of nights were disturbed because Paul and I were messing about, so on the third night, Perry decided to bring his mattress into our room and sleep on the floor. I was never certain whether it was to keep an eye on us or because Paul had told him his room was haunted.

After a couple of days Paul could see that I wasn't my usual bubbly self. I eventually confessed to him about my money situation. I had only a fiver left to last two weeks, as I had spent all my holiday money on Helen before we had gone away. Paul, being a top bloke, knew I was worried about telling Perry, who would have lectured me on the benefits of saving. Paul and Perry held a high-level house meeting regarding my predicament and decided to lend me a tenner each, so that I could resume enjoying my holiday.

It sounds silly now, but I was really concerned about what those guys thought about me. I had very little self-esteem at the time. They were top mates for doing that, and it meant a lot. In Chrissy world, £20 was an awful lot of money, so I was back to being a happy chappie. I could worry about paying them back when I got home.

Paul was in a relationship with a lovely girl named Carol, so he was obviously not going to stray. Perry was single, and I was deeply in love with the love of my life, Helen. The following day Perry had organised a smashing ploughman's lunch at the local hostelry. When we entered the bar I noticed an 18 stone, 6 foot 4 inch landlord, a blond, buxom landlady and a very dark-skinned girl, who turned out to be their daughter. We had a couple of pints of lager, and my confidence as usual started to grow. The daughter struck up a conversation with me and we got on very well. I don't know how it happened but I agreed to meet her in the local nightclub that evening. I will blame alcohol, yes, that's what I will do.

That night Paul, Perry and I went into the pub for a drink before we went to the nightclub. The giant, previously friendly, landlord was now not so friendly. His daughter had told him that she was meeting me in the nightclub, and that was that. His tone was almost menacing. He suggested to the three of us that we should go and spend the remainder of our holiday on the moors. I actually thought he was being a little over protective.

The boys and I went to the club and were stopped by the menacing bouncers. They tried to intimidate me into being abusive. They questioned me about my age. They were right, I was underage, but I had Paul's provisional driving licence on me. It didn't take long to find out from my new lady friend that the bouncers were mates with her father. They had been trying to warn me off. The strange thing was that I hadn't even been on. When they finally decided to let me into the club, I met up with my new lovely dark-skinned friend and discovered her name was Kim. We got on very well and the drinks flowed. I momentarily forgot that I was wasting my newly borrowed spending money and that I was deeply in love with Helen. I now think that I may have been a little drunk and was showing off with my new-found confidence. I thought that is how real men behaved. What a w***** I was.

I spent the whole evening, until the early hours just kissing her. She was pretty, she was very nice, but she wasn't my Helen. I can truly say that I had no intention of sleeping with her, no matter what she said. Which was just as well because I discovered that she was only fourteen years old. She probably still slept in a bunk bed. In my defence, she did look older, and I did meet her in a pub. It was no wonder her father was such an angry sod. What was he doing letting his fourteen-year-old daughter go out with a guy almost four years older, whom he didn't know? I guess that's why the bouncers stared at me all night. I thought it was because they were jealous, but it seems they were monitoring a bloody sex offender, or so they thought. Fancy letting a bloody fourteen-year-old girl into a night club. It was bad enough allowing me in. That night I spent half of the money the boys had lent me.

The next day Perry had planned a day for the three of us to go to Paignton pier again. I thought it was a good idea to keep away from the pub. Lolita had a big crush on me and I didn't want to annoy her dad any more. As we stood on the pier I decided it would be a well worthwhile expense getting my fortune told. I thought that £3 was the wisest money I could ever spend. Madame Petrulengo confirmed that I was going to marry my current girlfriend and that we were going to have healthy, beautiful twin daughters. I was over the moon. I was told I was going to be a father without even visiting the doctor. I needed that good news to keep me going. I then realised that I had to let Kim down gently and I knew I had been foolish.

Later that day we returned to the local pub, and I hoped to get the opportunity to have a quick word with Kim, away from her mum and dad. She was already there waiting for me, with her mum and dad nearby. She was infatuated with me, and her parents seemed to let her spend time with me. I suppose they were trying to protect their daughter, but still allow her to develop and grow. All that I knew was that if I ditched her in the pub, after snogging her the night before, her giant father would have severely damaged me.

This left me with no alternative but to ignore the severity of the situation, and I took the coward's way out. I thought that I could last the next nine days by just being nice to her, and then I could just let her down gently. That would be the safest option, or so I thought. Unfortunately, she didn't see it that way. She couldn't keep her hands off me. She even tried to kiss me in front of her parents. Don't get me wrong, she kissed just fine, but I was in love with Helen, and Kim was just fourteen.

The next day Paul, Perry and I went into Plymouth. We wandered around the vast city and found ourselves down Union Street, not knowing that the street was notorious for prostitutes, bar room brawls, and sailors and marines from all over the world. We were just looking for an amusement arcade. We wandered aimlessly down that road until we stumbled across a seedy-looking tattoo parlour. It was named Doc Price's Tattoo Shop. I thought it must be okay as it was run by a man from the medical profession.

Because the fortune teller confirmed that I was getting married to Helen, I wanted to cement my love with a tattoo. I could see Perry and Paul shaking their heads and disapproving of my choice. But hey, I was in love. I chose the biggest tattoo

I could afford and sat in the chair. When the needle first went into my arm I nearly flew through the ceiling. I thought he was doing it wrong because it hurt so much. How could anything legal be so painful? After thirty minutes of sheer agony I had a beautiful swallow tattooed on the top of my right arm. It was a work of art. I willingly gave him seven of my last eight pounds. I was nearly back to being skint again.

At that point I think the three of us were getting on each other's nerves. We all wanted to do different things and we were tired. Paul and I decided to go into a porn shop and buy some seedy underwear for our girlfriends; Perry was really bored with us. We both fingered through the underwear for what seemed an eternity. I don't remember what Paul bought for Carol but I went for some red crotchless, tasteless, nylon knickers. They were probably the tackiest knickers I had ever seen, or have ever seen since. I had holes in my pants and they were hardly considered sexy. But those awful knickers cost me my last pound.

After that last blow out, we all decided to go home. We actually went home a week early. I then had the problem of parting with my new, young female friend. I had two choices. I could be honest and tell her the truth, that I was in a relationship, or I could go home and ignore her telephone calls forever. It could never have worked out between us. I was used to girls dancing around their handbags, not their satchels. And anyway, according to Madame Petrulengo I was going to marry and father twins with Helen. I am not proud of the fact that I went home like the Cowardly Lion, and I never returned any of her calls. In my meagre defence though, I did not have any physical relationship with her. I never did give Helen those awful red knickers; I left them in a brown paper bag at Mrs B's house, much to Micky's disgust. I soon realised that karma was to play a big part in my life.

Paul and I thought we were cool in this picture.
Perry wouldn't have one taken with us.

Chapter 31

The little red hotel

Get some rest,
Sleep like a log.
Nothing's so cosy,
As a lovely, wet dog.

As the weeks went past they felt like years. All of my experiences were new ones and it felt exciting. I finally left the steelworks and those months had felt like decades. I was so glad to be away from the bullying.

I got a job with the government stores at the depot where I had nearly drowned. I am not sure it was the wisest of moves as I had a lot of sad memories of that place. Every day was a constant reminder of our family tragedy. But having a job was important, and the people were decent. I enjoyed their stories. The old boys had all served in the forces during the war or the Home Guard. The ladies had served in the munitions factories, service, or the Land Army. They were incredible people and treated me well. There was regular overtime and I could earn a lot more money. On a good week I could earn three to four times more than at the steelworks.

That meant a whole new world opened up for me. If I worked hard then I could go out partying Thursday night,

Friday night, Saturday night and Sunday night. Plus I paid my mother more rent, had enough to buy new clothes and my favourite Benson and Hedges cigarettes. I had risen from No 6 to Bensons and I considered myself to have gone up a class, ha ha ha.

The time was getting closer for Helen to go off to university and I hadn't really thought our relationship through. She was way too good for me, and I was boxing well above my weight. I eventually met her mother, father and little sister and I couldn't believe what I saw. They were extremely well-spoken, and they had a massive great house situated in acres of land. They had a tennis court and an indoor swimming pool, too.

When Helen had first told me about her house on a little estate I had thought she meant a council-type estate, not a family-owned estate. Her mother and father were best friends with her previous boyfriend's parents. I didn't really have a chance. I could see that Helen felt sorry for me. Her father totally ignored me and didn't want me in the house. Her mum tried to be polite but she was under the watchful eye of her husband. As far as he was concerned I had split up Helen and her boyfriend, and I was nothing more than a peasant. I treated them with total respect; I even thanked them for their hospitality. (It seemed that my dad had taught me something far more important than class, status and wealth, he had taught me good manners, and I will be eternally grateful for that.) Helen's father was an extremely rude man.

At one visit to see Helen I had to stay at her friend's house, and the parents were doctors. They were the total opposite; they were lovely and kind, but I was still a fish out of water. I just felt so out of place and awkward.

One memorable weekend back home I got an invite from a couple of local lads to go clubbing with them in Daventry. I was still under age but that didn't matter. Both lads were older: Trev was a carpenter and twenty years old and Freddy was a mechanic. He was twenty-six years old. Helen was away at some university induction programme that I wasn't interested in, which was just as well because they never invited me. In those days I thought that only posh kids who were too lazy to get jobs went to university. I was a local lad who had narrow-minded and blinkered views. The previous week I had bought a new cream suit, a couple of shirts and a pair of Levi cream leather shoes from Mrs B's catalogue. Mrs B kindly turned the trousers up, and with a trendy, freshly cut hair style I thought I looked gorgeous. Or as gorgeous as a 5-feet 4-inch, seventeen-year-old boy could be.

That night out was to be another exciting new experience. The three of us got a taxi into Daventry and visited a couple of bars, and then to a club they knew. It was wonderful and I felt like somebody. The other two were also extremely well turned out. Fred wore a dark suit and narrow tie and Trev wore dark trousers and a white jacket. We all had highlights in our hair, and Fred and I had the Clark Gable pencil moustache. Fred, being older, carried that look well. I, being younger, looked more like Betty Grable. We weren't bad-looking lads, admittedly on varying scales, with me at the latter end.

While we were in the club we chatted to loads of girls, danced with some of them, and drank until the club closed. Girls came up to us, and we spent money like water. I was terribly naive. Those girls knew how to play a young guy, and I was serving my nightclub apprenticeship. Fred may retell the following story a little differently than Trev and I, but this is how I remember it.

At about 2:00 A.M. we left the nightclub a little worse for wear. Between the three of us we did not have enough money for a taxi, and Fred was our only hope. He knew lots of people in Daventry, so he could borrow money for our taxi home. While Trev and I urinated up the side of a rundown building, a girl walked past and started to talk to Fred. They then walked off and spent a cosy remainder of the night together at her flat. It was as quick as that, which left Trev and

I stuck in Daventry, dressed like characters from Saturday Night Fever. We didn't have any warm clothing, we didn't have any money and we didn't have any transport. As Trev was older, I left him with total responsibility for getting us out of Daventry alive. To me it may as well have been the Congo. Four miles from home is a bloody long way when you are cold, drunk and tired. To top it off it started raining. Trev had the brilliant idea that we should get into a telephone box, the one that stands by the road that runs out of Daventry towards Weedon.

We huddled in that tiny phone box, soaking wet, and my brand new suit was crumpled. Trev had another great idea. He said that we should rip every page out of the telephone directories, screw each page into a ball, and then stuff them down each other's shirts, jackets and trousers. We padded each other out like Michelin men and tried to get warm. My lovely cream suit was now well and truly ruined, and so was his white jacket. Our attire was completely wet and covered in ink from the directories.

We huddled together on the floor of the telephone box and fell into a drunken sleep. Around 4:00 A.M., I heard a noise outside, so I rubbed the steam from a window pane and saw a beautiful sight. It was a large, golden Labrador with a waggy tail and a big smiley face. Our eyes met and we became instant friends. I decided to let the little beauty into the kiosk. He was obviously lost, very wet and very smelly. I noticed that he had a name tag around his neck: he was called 'Zac'. We soon decided that our new-found furry friend could cuddle up on top of us both. That hairy fellow kept us both warm.

At about 5:00 A.M., while we were deep in slumber, there was a loud knock on the kiosk door. All the windows were completely steamed up, so I said the first thing that came into my head, in a very welcoming voice, "Who is it"? The reply was not quite so friendly: "It is the police here, sir". At that point Zac went barmy: he was jumping all over us, barking and trying to get at our blue-suited visitors. I had to hold him by his collar to stop him biting them. Fortunately one of the police officers passed me a dog lead and instructed me to calm down Zac and put him into the back of their police car. My new best friend was loaded into the car, and he looked sad. I gave him a hug and a stroke and said goodbye. I never saw him again.

By that time the policemen had taken a good look at Trev and me, and they were trying to hold back tears of amusement. One of them had to walk away biting his bottom lip. Something had tickled their fancy. It wasn't until I looked at Trev that I realised what was so funny. We both had hair sticking up, we were covered in ink, paw prints all over us, and we were padded out like sumo wrestlers. And to top it off we had been asleep in a telephone box with a large dog. As God is my witness the following happened. One of the crying policemen picked up his radio and issued the following statement, "We have found your dog, Sarge, and he has been asleep in a telephone box with two youths". It was only the police sergeant's bloody dog, who had decided to run away, desert, go AWOL from the force. The mickey-taking coppers then gave us a lecture and told us to walk home. Being such law abiding citizens we waited until they drove away then re-entered our sleeping place. By 8:00 A.M., we managed to get a bus home.

The following weekend I introduced Trev to my beloved Helen, but that was not to be such a happy time. Trev and I and a couple of the lads had been drinking and Helen wanted to talk about something very serious. She sensibly decided to break up with me. She had been getting pressure from her parents, and she was going off to university. She was a different class from me, but I was devastated. When she said goodbye I burst into tears; I sobbed like a baby. Fortunately, Trev had drunk sufficient amounts of Holsten Pils, that he also burst into tears. That wound took a very long time to heal, but it was my Karma. The last I heard about Helen was that she followed her father's wishes and married her sailor boyfriend.

It seems that Madame Petrulengo's prediction was a little wayward. I wonder if I can get my money back? I have to say that I do miss that dog Zac very much.

I obviously don't have any pictures of Zac, so I thought I would add some pictures of my dog Pippin. She is the happiest dog in the world.

Pippin on the Queen's birthday.

Pippin doing her Mother Teresa impression.

Chapter 32

Return to Devon

Get the girl,
Do be quick.
Before she's taken,
Or covered in sick.

Who would have thought it? A few months later my brother Andrew returned home on leave and announced he was to marry. He was nineteen years old, but the military had matured him very quickly. He had met a lovely RAF girl who was stationed at RAF Halton. She was slightly older than Andrew, and had a thick Devon accent. They announced they were to have a military wedding and it was to take place in her hometown of Tavistock, Devon.

Fortunately, Andrew had invited Trev who was an old classmate of his from school, and a local lad, Steve. That meant I could get a lift in Steve's car, and share the petrol costs. Unfortunately, my brother Neville and his girlfriend were also squashed in the car, and the five of us headed down to Devon.

That five-hour journey took forever. Neville and I bickered all the way, and it had gone well beyond sibling rivalry. So much so that two weeks previously Neville had returned home very, very drunk and started shouting at my mother. I got out of bed and told him to leave her alone. He went into a rage and rammed my head into a wardrobe door, rendering me unconscious. My mother called the police, who jumped on him and calmed him down. My mother decided not to press charges against him. I have a feeling that if it had been me attacking one of my siblings, then I would still be locked up.

We eventually arrived in Tavistock, and booked ourselves into a bed and breakfast. It was very basic, and I had to share a room with Trev and Steve. We organised to meet up with all of Andrew's service mates and have a right good stag night. Trev, Steve and Neville went straight onto the scrumpy cider, but I drunk the much weaker lager. I wanted to pace myself, and anyway I had my eye on one of the service women. There is something about a woman in uniform. Unfortunately, Neville was never renowned for holding his drink.

We soon got into the party spirit, and after a couple of hours Neville started squabbling with Andrew. Andrew was not going to be belittled in front of his military buddies, and I knew it could quite easily come to blows. Neville was struggling to accept that his younger brothers were growing up. After a number of the guys had told Neville to calm down, he stumbled off in a drunken huff. The scrumpy cider had claimed its first casualty. At that point the hen party was fully merged with our stag party, and I was fancying my chances with the little Welsh service girl.

The evening was moving along fine. I sat across the table from Trev, right next to that very pretty girl. She told me that she thought civilian guys were usually immature, but that we were a welcome change. When I looked across at Trev, I noticed his eyes bulging like a giant frog, and his cheeks puffing out. He then decided to projectile vomit across the table, filling up an ash tray and all over the lovely girl that I was chatting up. She was covered in cider-flavoured vomit, and it stank. I was now completely blown out, as I was guilty by association. I behaved responsibly and began cleaning up Trev's sick with bar towels, and he did the honourable thing. He ran off and locked himself in the gents' toilet. That scrumpy had claimed its second victim.

Trev spent the remainder of that evening locked in the toilet cubicle, far too embarrassed to come out. I eventually managed to convince him that nobody had seen him being ill, and that nobody would say a word. When he finally exited the loo everyone cheered, and it was hilarious. I would have found it even funnier if I hadn't smelled of sick.

The next day was the wedding day, and Neville had not been seen since he stormed off from the pub. We eventually found out that he had got lost, then couldn't get into the bed and breakfast and decided to sleep behind a churchyard wall. The ironic thing was that it was the same church Andrew was to be married in. I suppose it saved him paying out for a taxi. The tension was still felt in the church during the service. So much so that when the vicar read out the bit about, "Does anyone object to the marriage, speak now or forever hold your peace", we all looked at Neville.

Instead all we heard was a very excited little David whispering to me at the top of his voice, in an echoing church. His words will haunt me forever. He looked towards our new in-laws and bellowed, "See that girl with the really big teeth? She is going to be related to you".

Chapter 33

Football legends

You can play for us,
Get your own team.
We all pulled together,
And started our dream.

I was very proud to be a village boy, a country boy, or to be more precise, a Weedon boy. The majority of us lads had grown up together; we had played football together in the streets and we had fought together. Some of us even shared the same girlfriends, namely Micky and I. When my dad died, Micky let me kiss his girlfriend, which was very kind of him because I wouldn't have done the same for him. I would never have seen them again, as he was extremely well endowed. I wish I had been a little older when Dad died as I would have had far more sympathy sex.

Evening times were fine for us local lads as we all went to the pubs together, or sometimes to the nightclubs. Our main aims were to get drunk and find women, or should I say girls, or probably both. The majority of us were just basic creatures. Like most young men, we lied about our exploits. If we got a kiss, we said a grope. When we got a grope, we managed to turn that into full sex, and so it went on.

Weekend daytime was a different kettle of fish. We would all wake up with hangovers on Saturday morning and then meet up at the Globe Hotel for a pint, which was situated on the main road in Weedon. Even though I was underage, my moustache was the equivalent of an ID card now. As far as the owners were concerned we were well dressed, we all worked, we were respectful, we were well behaved most of the time and we spent lots of money.

One Saturday Micky, Trev, Paul, Bebsy, Perry, Pluto, Belly and I met up for our lunchtime drink. We all drank, five of us smoked, and we all had hangovers and felt like crap. We were turning into old men before our very eyes. In those days, like in most pubs, hotels and clubs up and down the country the subject turned to football. We had played a lot of football as kids, and some of us had represented our school, and we played for the local youth team. Micky was in a different class, as he had been on trials for Aston Villa. With the right direction and passion he could have made it, and if he hadn't started drinking and smoking from an early age, that might have helped, too. When he went for his trials he treated it as if it were a holiday. That day, after our first pint we unanimously decided we should stop drinking Saturday lunchtimes, and get ourselves a lot fitter.

As quick as a flash we all rushed home to get into our

old football shorts, shirts and boots. We looked a right sorry state; we looked like evacuees walking onto the jubilee football field. The only difference was that we didn't have gas masks and nametags. To us, though, we were Toshack, Keegan, Chivers, Peters, Jennings, Reaney and Coates. We spent the next hour running around re-living our childhoods. We had spent so much of our time trying to be adults that we had forgotten what we had loved.

It was Bebsy who said that we hadn't forgotten our old skills, and that we should start a football team. Weedon already had an adult's football team, and they were flying high in the league. Some of us had tried to join the team, but it was too close-knit, and we weren't welcome. They didn't want seventeen and eighteen year old kids playing, as they were all in their twenties and thirties.

When we went back to the Globe Hotel covered in mud and stinking of sweat, we sat around the bar area table, drank a couple of pints, and had a well-earned smoke. We were excitable captains of industry, as we were going to start our own football club. We could picture the sporting history books stating when the Old Etonians were formed, when Blackpool won the F.A. Cup, when Liverpool had done the double, when Wales got to the quarter final of the 1958 World Cup, and when the WEEDON GLOBETROTTERS were formed.

We wanted to call ourselves the Weedon Globetrotters. We had spent two hours thinking up a name; now all we needed was a pitch to play on, a team strip, opposition teams, nets, goalposts and at least twelve good local lads to be in our squad. All that would cost us a lot of money. The hotel at the time was owned by Keith and Gina and another couple named Anne and Arthur. They were very nice people who treated us extremely well. We casually mentioned to Arthur that we were going to name our new football team after his hotel and he was delighted.

Straight away he asked if we needed any help and support; we had landed him on our first attempt. Before we left the hotel that afternoon we were promised sponsorship for our football strips. Now we had to approach the mighty Weedon Football Club. We politely asked if we could share the pitch with them, use their line marking equipment and borrow their goalposts and nets. We knew they were a Sunday team; therefore, would have to enter a Saturday league. They said no. It was like a Manchester United versus Manchester City scenario, and they wanted nothing to do with us urchins. We were a little surprised because we were all local lads, and very few members of the Weedon team were local. We then decided to put money into the team ourselves and we bought our own equipment.

Fortunately, we had Carol (Paul's girlfriend). She took over all the fixture lists, paperwork and all the complicated stuff; she was our brains. She sorted out getting permission from the council to use the pitch on Saturday, much to our local rival's disgust.

We looked at buying the goalposts, but they were far too expensive. We then decided that Trev, who had recently completed his carpentry apprenticeship, could make them. Everyone had a role to fulfil, and being blokes we left it until the last minute, hoping that someone else would do it.

The day arrived for our first home game, and the goalposts were still not made. They were just two long bits of plain wood. We made Trev get up early on the Saturday and begin work on them. Paul was in charge of white-washing the lines, Bebs sorted out the changing rooms, Carol and the girls (they weren't called WAGS then) sorted out the refreshments, and Micky and I had been entrusted to gloss paint the posts, after Trev had made them.

On reflection, that was probably not a very good idea, as we both had short attention spans. Micky was busy painting one of the uprights when I had a brilliant idea. I noticed that his Levi jeans were looking very snug and sexy around his bottom cheeks, and it was too good an opportunity to miss. I dipped my stubby hand into the paint pot and placed it on his backside, leaving a perfect handprint. He was furious at my wonderful piece of artwork, and picked up one of the paint pots and stuck it on my head. I was completely covered in gloss paint. The other lads noticed the fracas and relieved us of our duties.

Thirty minutes later the referee arrived, just as we had attached the nets to the posts. The paint was still tacky and my head and face were a brilliant gloss white. I had to play ninety minutes of football, looking like an albino, sweating underneath a thick coat of paint. But just for the record, we won that game.

Our first season was fantastic. We became much fitter, and we enjoyed ourselves. We were a band of brothers. About eight games into the season, we played against a team called Brington. They were situated on the edge of the Althorp Estate where Princess Diana lived. I felt fit, we had a good side out, and I was our second-highest goal scorer, after Micky, of course. But as a 5-feet 4-inch striker, I wasn't too bad.

We lined up for the kick-off, and my jaw hit the ground. I noticed that a member of the team was one of the bullies from the steelworks, and to make matters worse he was marking me. For the first five minutes I ran rings around him, and it felt wonderful. I remember thinking that brains beat brawn. Our goalkeeper Woody sent one of his big kicks up the middle of the field, and I went for the ball. As I did, 16 stone of solid bully hit my ribcage. He stuck his elbow under my ribs and completely clattered me. All the air left my body, and I thought I was having a heart attack, or at least had a punctured lung. I was left lying on the grass pitch gasping for breath, dying. (Okay, that is a little over dramatic, but that's how it felt.)

Some say that when soldiers are injured they shout for their mothers, and as I am constantly reminded by the others, my final death gasps were, "Micky, Micky, Micky". The referee blew his whistle and all our team started laughing. I could have been dying, and all they did was laugh. I was carried off and tended to by Carol; she was also our physio.

A couple of weeks later we played against Kislingbury, and the goalkeeper was a head case. He clattered me and I didn't even have the ball. That would have been another early bath, if one had been fitted in the changing room. It seems that these days everyone gets yellow or red cards, but it very rarely happened then.

A week after that fiasco we found ourselves playing against another tough ale-house team. We were doing well in the league and the unexpected happened. The referee was having a pretty bad game, and there was a lot of backchat from the players. Micky decided it was okay to call him a f******* w*****. The ref stopped the game and gave him a red card. Micky spent the next five minutes going up to each of us telling us he had been sent off. He was in shock, as he had played from a very early age and had never even been booked. It was hilarious seeing him near to tears. As usual, my joy at his demise was short lived. Because ten minutes later I went in for a tackle, and while I was down on the ground, an opposition player decided to stamp on my hand with his football studs. I was again in agony, and Carol again tended my injury and took me off to hospital.

I was so shy at the hospital that I wouldn't let the nurses take off my football shirt because Carol was in the room. I was very prim about some things, and undressing was one of them. The nurses weren't too happy about plastering over a broken hand while I was still clothed. I arrived back at the Globe Hotel with a plastered arm and still in my football kit. I thought that I would get a hero's welcome, but all I got was abuse and laughter.

Chapter 34

All mouth, no trousers

Where is Chris?
Where are his clothes?
He's in the wardrobe,
And his clothes are all froze.

As we were typical, young working class men (well, teenagers),
we all had some experience, some encounters with the
opposite sex. But really we were all very inexperienced, apart
from Micky, and I was probably the most. I could only
communicate confidently with women if I had a few drinks
first; I lacked total self-esteem. Sometimes I would come
across as being arrogant and cocky, but it was all a facade. Our
aim was to work hard, earn money, get nice clothes, go out
drinking and go to bed with women. Ninety percent of the
time that did not happen. Unfortunately we would get too
drunk, and back then the majority of women seemed to have
restraint. I discovered that the more alcohol I consumed the
higher standard of female I aimed for, and this led me to
aiming a little too high. Put it this way, if I had been a Spitfire
pilot during the war I wouldn't have crossed out many Focke
Wulfe's on the side of my aeroplane. But as drunken dwarves
go I held my own. Perhaps a little too often some may say.

I certainly had my bluff called on one certain Saturday night. My mates Steve, Nick, Ady and I were invited to a house party in Daventry. Before we went to the house with our bottles we decided to have a couple of drinks. We went to the Beachcomber pub and then to the Old Swiss Cottage bar. The vibe felt good: I had a fresh haircut, good clothes and I didn't have any spots, which was always a bonus when out on the pull. Usually in Daventry you had to watch your back, because you could quite easily chat up the wrong girl. Even making eye contact with the wrong person could have got you a broken nose. Many a time we ended up in a scrape because of poor judgement, and many a time I had been punched in the face for talking to someone's girlfriend, wife or sister. It was a bloody minefield out there.

We were having a nice evening in the Swiss Cottage, and there seemed to be far more women than men. I looked towards the bar area and noticed a very attractive female looking at me, so I gave her the old Griffo smile. I probably looked slightly retarded, but it seemed to work. She approached me and introduced herself as Beverley. She was very pretty, well groomed, mid twenties (about eight years older than I) and very, very confident. She knew exactly what she wanted, and she wanted me, yes, little old me. (You have to remember that my greatest sexual conquests were in my head.)

She told me straight away that she fancied me and she wanted to go to the house party with me. Incredibly she couldn't keep her hands off me, and she was hornier than anyone I had ever known. As soon as we arrived at the house she was kissing me, touching me, and frightening the bloody life out of me. My alter ego would not have had any problem, but me, I was petrified. I drank as much as I could to gain the courage, but no matter how much I drank I just couldn't become brave. Don't get me wrong, I did fancy her and I was extremely aroused, but she terrified me. The final straw was when she looked into my eyes and said she was ready, I thought, "Ready for what"? She then took my stubby little hand and walked towards the staircase. She was taking me to bed, to use me for her pleasure.

I don't know why I did the following, but I did. She went into the bedroom and started removing her clothes very sexily, and then she got into bed. I gulped and said I was going to the bathroom, and that I would return in a couple of minutes. I did go to the bathroom, and then I quietly went into one of the other bedrooms, climbed into the wardrobe, covered myself with heaps of clothes and fell into a very deep sleep.

I woke up the next morning to the amusement of all the other house guests who had stayed over. Fortunately for me Beverley had gone home many hours before. I felt and still feel terrible. I was a coward and everyone knew it. They were calling me Wardrobe Willy and Wardrobe W*****, and many other derogatory names, but hey, I deserved it.

When you are a teenager every week is a new adventure. There are new experiences, new people to meet, and no two weeks are the same. A couple of weeks later a few of us decided to return to Daventry. There was Nick, Trev, a few other guys and me. We were invited to another party at the house of a girl named Debbie. I suggested we should avoid the Swiss Cottage for obvious reasons.

Trev had met a new girl the previous week, and he had decided that we were to meet her at the Beachcomber pub. That should have been a nice experience, but when Trev introduced me to her my jaw hit the ground. She looked at me, and I went bright red. It was Beverley. Yes, Beverley, the girl who caused me to hide in the wardrobe. I never asked Trev how he felt, but his excessive drinking that night might have been a clue.

We eventually went to the house party and more drink flowed. I was on my best behaviour because I didn't want to make a fool of myself again, not in such a short space of time. At about midnight I looked towards the sofa and there was Trev, fast asleep, drunk, his mouth wide open, and he was dribbling. That left me with no alternative. I decided to use a thick marker pen and draw a big black moustache and beard on his face.

By that time I had noticed that Beverley was extremely angry with him. That gave me the perfect opportunity to apologise. I explained everything to her. I told her the truth: I told her that I had been nervous, had felt inadequate, that I didn't have any confidence, and that I had even less bedroom experience. She again took my hand and guided me to the bedroom, and there she promised to be gentle with me. You know what? I played the innocent, lack of experience card many times after that. I realised that girls didn't always want the confident type but they were happier with the gentler, inexperienced type. I was happier being a beta male; anyway, it was too much hassle being an alpha male, far too much responsibility and too many fights. True to her word, Beverley was gentle with me; in fact it was rather pleasant.

Beverley and I were engaged in a very steamy embrace when the door burst open. It was Trev. He had woken up from his very drunken slumber and had gone looking for Bev, and then for me. At that point most guys would have punched their friend in the face, or screamed, or shouted, but Trev didn't. He actually tried to get into bed with us. I howled with laughter, but Bev started screaming. She was having none of it. Trev then decided to pick up all of my clothes off the bedroom floor and wear them over the top of his. He put on my pants, socks, trousers and shirt and then marched off. I eventually found my trousers and shirt in the freezer, frozen solid, and I have no idea where my pants and socks ended up.

Chapter 35

Farewell my valley

Time to go,
Time to part.
Gone are my friends,
Left is my heart.

Like every situation in life there is an end—an end to the good
and an end to the bad. Weedon had been my only world. I
believed I knew everything about everyone in it, and I believed
that they knew everything about me. I was considered by many
to be a happy lad, always messing about and always laughing.
What they didn't realise was that my mind was in turmoil. I
hadn't properly grieved about the deaths in my family, and I
had bottled everything up into my tiny mind. No-one saw my
emotions; they were mine. At night when I lay alone in my bed
my demons would arrive in my bedroom. But during the day I
worked, played and had begun serious drinking at least five
nights a week. Alcohol was my sleeping companion.

Throughout my life, my mother had always
threatened to move away. She never had, so I assumed she
never would. She had been in Weedon for more than thirty
years, and I assumed that she would eventually end her days
there. I just carried on working, paying my rent, and just

getting on with my life. Every single day she would say she was moving, and every single day I would brush it aside as an idle threat. She knew that by moving away I would be hurt, unsettled and totally alone, or at least that is what I believed. I though she wanted to punish me. She probably didn't, but that's how I felt. There was almost venom in her voice, and I felt totally alone and dejected. Looking back, I think I was acting like a spoilt child for feeling that way. I know there is a time for a bird to leave the nest, but I would rather it was taught to fly first. I was an emotional, unstable wreck, but I kept it well hidden.

One Friday night after I returned home from work, I ate my dinner and had my usual red-hot bath. It was the end of the week, and I felt good. I listened to the usual "Friday on my mind" by David Bowie, as I dressed to go out. I put on my red tights, a green velvet smock, and a green hat. I then added some plastic ears and nose, and, to top it off, green shoes with bells on them. I was going to be a Pixie.

Some bright spark at the Weedon Globetrotters Football Club had decided on setting up a fundraiser. Each football player would be dressed as a Pixie and would be tied to one of the local girls, also dressed in the same attire. They would then run three legged around all the drinking establishments in the village, and both had to consume an alcoholic drink in each place. That meant at least fifteen footballers being tied to fifteen girls. The boy was matched with the girl by pulling names out of a bag. I still think it was rigged, as I ended up with a girl named Tracey. I hope she doesn't mind me saying but she was loud and of a similar height to me. On the plus side, though, she could hold her drink. But I have to say that because of our stature we did look like real Pixies.

We began at the Globe Hotel and ran to the Crossroads. We were given a five-minute gap between each couple. Tracey and I started first and arrived at the posh Crossroads Hotel. We went to the bar and ordered our first drink.

I necked a pint of lager and Tracey drank a half. It was brilliant, as it had been arranged that we were to have free drinks at each establishment. We then had to run two miles alongside the A5 main road, the old Roman road called Watling Street, to the Narrow Boat public house. Again I had a pint and Tracey had another half. By that time I felt bloated and out of breath. Smoking, drinking and running was not a good combination. My plastic nose was cutting off my oxygen supply and I had to breathe in and out from my mouth.

The next part of the journey was running from the Narrow Boat down to the Malsters Arms, which was about another two miles. I then had to drink another pint of lager there and Tracey had to push me. From there we ran a couple of hundred yards up to the Conservative Club and have yet another pint and a half. I felt very rough by that time. When we left the Conservative Club to run down to the Plume of Feathers pub I started to get the taste of vomit in my mouth. More worryingly was the fact that every other Pixie couple were overtaking us. They passed us on the way from the Club to the Plume and I couldn't understand why. I was a pretty fast drinker, and we weren't the slowest of runners, so we should have been in the top half of the teams.

While we were in the Plume of Feathers I decided to sip my pint, rather than gulp it, as it was difficult keeping it down. The only way to stop myself being sick during the remainder of the race was to walk the next leg. We walked from the Plume on the mile-and-a-half journey up to the New Inn public house, where there we drank another very slow pint and a half of lager. We staggered from there, across the main road to the Wheatsheaf pub, and at that point I was close to passing out. We finished our drinks and half-walked and half-crawled back to the original starting point of the Globe Hotel. We saw our imaginary finishing line and just felt so relieved.

We entered the Globe Hotel in completely last position, way after every other team had finished. We ordered our final drinks and it was only at that point that I realised why we were so far behind everybody else and why I felt so incredibly ill. I was informed by Arthur, the hotel owner, that every male Pixie only had to drink half a pint of lager in each pub. I foolishly had drunk a complete pint in each pub, and no-one told me differently. I drank eight pints of strong lager, ran about seven miles, smoked a few cigarettes, and had my oxygen supply limited by my plastic nose.

My final dash after that last pint of the race was into the gents' toilet, where I threw up all eight pints. My plastic nose flew off and went down the toilet pan, never to be seen again. Within a few minutes, after wiping off the sick from my face, I was back with the boys partying. We had a cracking night and raised more than £500 for the old people's Christmas party and our beloved Weedon Globetrotters Football Club. We would have made even more money, but Micky decided to spend his sponsorship money on alcohol and cigarettes instead.

That night I wandered home after midnight, still dressed in my Pixie outfit. When I entered the house, I noticed a note on top of the kitchen table. It read, "Chris, I've got a job as a warden of an old people's home and will be moving in four weeks time. There will not be room for you to move with us. Mum".

I never slept that night, and I raced downstairs when I heard my mother get up to let the dogs out. I began by asking her all the important questions. She told me that Neville and his girlfriend were buying a place and moving away. My mother was moving to another county with little Ceri and little David and she was taking the dogs, cats and birds with her, but there wasn't any room at the inn for me. That really hurt, not because I was going to be on my own but because I felt rejected. I didn't want a hug; I just wanted some words of encouragement. Instead, all I heard from her was, "You won't find anywhere for the money you give me each week".

I telephoned the local council and asked if I could take over the rent on our council house, and pay all of the bills myself. I explained that I was a local lad, had no criminal convictions, and I held a steady job. They very rudely informed me that it was a family council house and I didn't have any entitlement to it. The rude person said that if I didn't move out on the same day as my mother moved then they would evict me. For the first time in my life I felt sorry for myself; it felt that the whole bloody world was against me.

Well, my little bit of the world, anyway. I could feel myself falling farther and farther into an abyss, and it was getting darker and darker. People then didn't talk about their problems, not like they do now. I eventually found a tiny

223

room, within a house that was situated at the top of the village, on the new estate. It was a pokey little kid's room, which had cowboy and red Indian wallpaper. It was like being stuck in a cell. The people I shared the house with stole my food and didn't replace it. I drank more and more alcohol to ease my depression; I used to steal my housemates' spirits in retaliation for nicking my food.

One evening, the Weedon Globetrotters were playing a match against a neighbouring village side, so Paul came and picked me up in his car. I never told him or any of my teammates that I went onto the pitch that evening slightly tipsy. I had consumed a few large gin and tonics mixed with vodka before the game.

At that point I was in my late teens, and I now know that I was suffering from depression and psychological issues, and the beginning of a serious alcohol problem. If that had happened today I would perhaps have been given some help. But instead I decided to persuade my mother to let me stay with her, at the old people's home for a short while. That enabled me to get my papers processed and go through all the necessary medicals: I misguidedly decided that the wisest move for a depressed, psychologically scarred, apprentice alcoholic would be to enlist in Her Majesty's Forces. I left my valley forever.

… THE FUTURE HAD YET TO HAPPEN …

30506187R00130

Printed in Poland
by Amazon Fulfillment
Poland Sp. z o.o., Wrocław